C-698   CAREER EXAMINATION SERIES

This is your
PASSBOOK for...

Real Property Manager

Test Preparation Study Guide
Questions & Answers

COPYRIGHT NOTICE

This book is SOLELY intended for, is sold ONLY to, and its use is RESTRICTED to individual, bona fide applicants or candidates who qualify by virtue of having seriously filed applications for appropriate license, certificate, professional and/or promotional advancement, higher school matriculation, scholarship, or other legitimate requirements of education and/or governmental authorities.

This book is NOT intended for use, class instruction, tutoring, training, duplication, copying, reprinting, excerption, or adaptation, etc., by:

1) Other publishers
2) Proprietors and/or Instructors of "Coaching" and/or Preparatory Courses
3) Personnel and/or Training Divisions of commercial, industrial, and governmental organizations
4) Schools, colleges, or universities and/or their departments and staffs, including teachers and other personnel
5) Testing Agencies or Bureaus
6) Study groups which seek by the purchase of a single volume to copy and/or duplicate and/or adapt this material for use by the group as a whole without having purchased individual volumes for each of the members of the group
7) Et al.

Such persons would be in violation of appropriate Federal and State statutes.

PROVISION OF LICENSING AGREEMENTS – Recognized educational, commercial, industrial, and governmental institutions and organizations, and others legitimately engaged in educational pursuits, including training, testing, and measurement activities, may address request for a licensing agreement to the copyright owners, who will determine whether, and under what conditions, including fees and charges, the materials in this book may be used them. In other words, a licensing facility exists for the legitimate use of the material in this book on other than an individual basis. However, it is asseverated and affirmed here that the material in this book CANNOT be used without the receipt of the express permission of such a licensing agreement from the Publishers. Inquiries re licensing should be addressed to the company, attention rights and permissions department.

All rights reserved, including the right of reproduction in whole or in part, in any form or by any means, electronic or mechanical, including photocopying, recording, or by any information storage and retrieval system, without permission in writing from the Publisher.

Copyright © 2025 by
National Learning Corporation

212 Michael Drive, Syosset, NY 11791
(516) 921-8888 • www.passbooks.com
E-mail: info@passbooks.com

PASSBOOK® SERIES

THE *PASSBOOK® SERIES* has been created to prepare applicants and candidates for the ultimate academic battlefield – the examination room.

At some time in our lives, each and every one of us may be required to take an examination – for validation, matriculation, admission, qualification, registration, certification, or licensure.

Based on the assumption that every applicant or candidate has met the basic formal educational standards, has taken the required number of courses, and read the necessary texts, the *PASSBOOK® SERIES* furnishes the one special preparation which may assure passing with confidence, instead of failing with insecurity. Examination questions – together with answers – are furnished as the basic vehicle for study so that the mysteries of the examination and its compounding difficulties may be eliminated or diminished by a sure method.

This book is meant to help you pass your examination provided that you qualify and are serious in your objective.

The entire field is reviewed through the huge store of content information which is succinctly presented through a provocative and challenging approach – the question-and-answer method.

A climate of success is established by furnishing the correct answers at the end of each test.

You soon learn to recognize types of questions, forms of questions, and patterns of questioning. You may even begin to anticipate expected outcomes.

You perceive that many questions are repeated or adapted so that you can gain acute insights, which may enable you to score many sure points.

You learn how to confront new questions, or types of questions, and to attack them confidently and work out the correct answers.

You note objectives and emphases, and recognize pitfalls and dangers, so that you may make positive educational adjustments.

Moreover, you are kept fully informed in relation to new concepts, methods, practices, and directions in the field.

You discover that you are actually taking the examination all the time: you are preparing for the examination by "taking" an examination, not by reading extraneous and/or supererogatory textbooks.

In short, this PASSBOOK®, used directedly, should be an important factor in helping you to pass your test.

REAL PROPERTY MANAGER

DUTIES:
Real Property Managers, under varying degrees of supervision, perform real property management, receivership, relocation and anti-abandonment work of varying degrees of difficulty in housing and other properties, and buildings owned, managed, or to be acquired by the City, or those at risk of being abandoned. Manage City-owned or receivership properties or supervise the management of buildings or developments financed by or leased from the City. Inspect and provide descriptions of properties. May operate a motor vehicle to travel to sites. All Real Property Managers perform related work.

SUBJECT OF EXAMINATION:
The written test is designed to test for knowledge, skills, and/or abilities in such areas as:
1. Real property management and tenant relocation procedures and practices;
2. Interpersonal relations;
3. Interviewing ;
4. Reading comprehension;
5. Filling out forms; and
6. Basic mathematics.

HOW TO TAKE A TEST

I. YOU MUST PASS AN EXAMINATION

A. *WHAT EVERY CANDIDATE SHOULD KNOW*

Examination applicants often ask us for help in preparing for the written test. What can I study in advance? What kinds of questions will be asked? How will the test be given? How will the papers be graded?

As an applicant for a civil service examination, you may be wondering about some of these things. Our purpose here is to suggest effective methods of advance study and to describe civil service examinations.

Your chances for success on this examination can be increased if you know how to prepare. Those "pre-examination jitters" can be reduced if you know what to expect. You can even experience an adventure in good citizenship if you know why civil service exams are given.

B. *WHY ARE CIVIL SERVICE EXAMINATIONS GIVEN?*

Civil service examinations are important to you in two ways. As a citizen, you want public jobs filled by employees who know how to do their work. As a job seeker, you want a fair chance to compete for that job on an equal footing with other candidates. The best-known means of accomplishing this two-fold goal is the competitive examination.

Exams are widely publicized throughout the nation. They may be administered for jobs in federal, state, city, municipal, town or village governments or agencies.

Any citizen may apply, with some limitations, such as the age or residence of applicants. Your experience and education may be reviewed to see whether you meet the requirements for the particular examination. When these requirements exist, they are reasonable and applied consistently to all applicants. Thus, a competitive examination may cause you some uneasiness now, but it is your privilege and safeguard.

C. *HOW ARE CIVIL SERVICE EXAMS DEVELOPED?*

Examinations are carefully written by trained technicians who are specialists in the field known as "psychological measurement," in consultation with recognized authorities in the field of work that the test will cover. These experts recommend the subject matter areas or skills to be tested; only those knowledges or skills important to your success on the job are included. The most reliable books and source materials available are used as references. Together, the experts and technicians judge the difficulty level of the questions.

Test technicians know how to phrase questions so that the problem is clearly stated. Their ethics do not permit "trick" or "catch" questions. Questions may have been tried out on sample groups, or subjected to statistical analysis, to determine their usefulness.

Written tests are often used in combination with performance tests, ratings of training and experience, and oral interviews. All of these measures combine to form the best-known means of finding the right person for the right job.

II. HOW TO PASS THE WRITTEN TEST

A. NATURE OF THE EXAMINATION

To prepare intelligently for civil service examinations, you should know how they differ from school examinations you have taken. In school you were assigned certain definite pages to read or subjects to cover. The examination questions were quite detailed and usually emphasized memory. Civil service exams, on the other hand, try to discover your present ability to perform the duties of a position, plus your potentiality to learn these duties. In other words, a civil service exam attempts to predict how successful you will be. Questions cover such a broad area that they cannot be as minute and detailed as school exam questions.

In the public service similar kinds of work, or positions, are grouped together in one "class." This process is known as *position-classification*. All the positions in a class are paid according to the salary range for that class. One class title covers all of these positions, and they are all tested by the same examination.

B. FOUR BASIC STEPS

1) Study the announcement

How, then, can you know what subjects to study? Our best answer is: "Learn as much as possible about the class of positions for which you've applied." The exam will test the knowledge, skills and abilities needed to do the work.

Your most valuable source of information about the position you want is the official exam announcement. This announcement lists the training and experience qualifications. Check these standards and apply only if you come reasonably close to meeting them.

The brief description of the position in the examination announcement offers some clues to the subjects which will be tested. Think about the job itself. Review the duties in your mind. Can you perform them, or are there some in which you are rusty? Fill in the blank spots in your preparation.

Many jurisdictions preview the written test in the exam announcement by including a section called "Knowledge and Abilities Required," "Scope of the Examination," or some similar heading. Here you will find out specifically what fields will be tested.

2) Review your own background

Once you learn in general what the position is all about, and what you need to know to do the work, ask yourself which subjects you already know fairly well and which need improvement. You may wonder whether to concentrate on improving your strong areas or on building some background in your fields of weakness. When the announcement has specified "some knowledge" or "considerable knowledge," or has used adjectives like "beginning principles of..." or "advanced ... methods," you can get a clue as to the number and difficulty of questions to be asked in any given field. More questions, and hence broader coverage, would be included for those subjects which are more important in the work. Now weigh your strengths and weaknesses against the job requirements and prepare accordingly.

3) Determine the level of the position

Another way to tell how intensively you should prepare is to understand the level of the job for which you are applying. Is it the entering level? In other words, is this the position in which beginners in a field of work are hired? Or is it an intermediate or advanced level? Sometimes this is indicated by such words as "Junior" or "Senior" in the class title. Other jurisdictions use Roman numerals to designate the level – Clerk I, Clerk II, for example. The word "Supervisor" sometimes appears in the title. If the level is not indicated by the title, check the description of duties. Will you be working under very close supervision, or will you have responsibility for independent decisions in this work?

4) Choose appropriate study materials

Now that you know the subjects to be examined and the relative amount of each subject to be covered, you can choose suitable study materials. For beginning level jobs, or even advanced ones, if you have a pronounced weakness in some aspect of your training, read a modern, standard textbook in that field. Be sure it is up to date and has general coverage. Such books are normally available at your library, and the librarian will be glad to help you locate one. For entry-level positions, questions of appropriate difficulty are chosen – neither highly advanced questions, nor those too simple. Such questions require careful thought but not advanced training.

If the position for which you are applying is technical or advanced, you will read more advanced, specialized material. If you are already familiar with the basic principles of your field, elementary textbooks would waste your time. Concentrate on advanced textbooks and technical periodicals. Think through the concepts and review difficult problems in your field.

These are all general sources. You can get more ideas on your own initiative, following these leads. For example, training manuals and publications of the government agency which employs workers in your field can be useful, particularly for technical and professional positions. A letter or visit to the government department involved may result in more specific study suggestions, and certainly will provide you with a more definite idea of the exact nature of the position you are seeking.

III. KINDS OF TESTS

Tests are used for purposes other than measuring knowledge and ability to perform specified duties. For some positions, it is equally important to test ability to make adjustments to new situations or to profit from training. In others, basic mental abilities not dependent on information are essential. Questions which test these things may not appear as pertinent to the duties of the position as those which test for knowledge and information. Yet they are often highly important parts of a fair examination. For very general questions, it is almost impossible to help you direct your study efforts. What we can do is to point out some of the more common of these general abilities needed in public service positions and describe some typical questions.

1) General information

Broad, general information has been found useful for predicting job success in some kinds of work. This is tested in a variety of ways, from vocabulary lists to questions about current events. Basic background in some field of work, such as sociology or economics, may be sampled in a group of questions. Often these are principles which have become familiar to most persons through exposure rather than through formal training. It is difficult to advise you how to study for these questions; being alert to the world around you is our best suggestion.

2) Verbal ability

An example of an ability needed in many positions is verbal or language ability. Verbal ability is, in brief, the ability to use and understand words. Vocabulary and grammar tests are typical measures of this ability. Reading comprehension or paragraph interpretation questions are common in many kinds of civil service tests. You are given a paragraph of written material and asked to find its central meaning.

3) Numerical ability

Number skills can be tested by the familiar arithmetic problem, by checking paired lists of numbers to see which are alike and which are different, or by interpreting charts and graphs. In the latter test, a graph may be printed in the test booklet which you are asked to use as the basis for answering questions.

4) Observation

A popular test for law-enforcement positions is the observation test. A picture is shown to you for several minutes, then taken away. Questions about the picture test your ability to observe both details and larger elements.

5) Following directions

In many positions in the public service, the employee must be able to carry out written instructions dependably and accurately. You may be given a chart with several columns, each column listing a variety of information. The questions require you to carry out directions involving the information given in the chart.

6) Skills and aptitudes

Performance tests effectively measure some manual skills and aptitudes. When the skill is one in which you are trained, such as typing or shorthand, you can practice. These tests are often very much like those given in business school or high school courses. For many of the other skills and aptitudes, however, no short-time preparation can be made. Skills and abilities natural to you or that you have developed throughout your lifetime are being tested.

Many of the general questions just described provide all the data needed to answer the questions and ask you to use your reasoning ability to find the answers. Your best preparation for these tests, as well as for tests of facts and ideas, is to be at your physical and mental best. You, no doubt, have your own methods of getting into an exam-taking mood and keeping "in shape." The next section lists some ideas on this subject.

IV. KINDS OF QUESTIONS

Only rarely is the "essay" question, which you answer in narrative form, used in civil service tests. Civil service tests are usually of the short-answer type. Full instructions for answering these questions will be given to you at the examination. But in case this is your first experience with short-answer questions and separate answer sheets, here is what you need to know:

1) Multiple-choice Questions

Most popular of the short-answer questions is the "multiple choice" or "best answer" question. It can be used, for example, to test for factual knowledge, ability to solve problems or judgment in meeting situations found at work.

A multiple-choice question is normally one of three types—
- It can begin with an incomplete statement followed by several possible endings. You are to find the one ending which *best* completes the statement, although some of the others may not be entirely wrong.
- It can also be a complete statement in the form of a question which is answered by choosing one of the statements listed.

- It can be in the form of a problem – again you select the best answer.

Here is an example of a multiple-choice question with a discussion which should give you some clues as to the method for choosing the right answer:

When an employee has a complaint about his assignment, the action which will *best* help him overcome his difficulty is to
   A. discuss his difficulty with his coworkers
   B. take the problem to the head of the organization
   C. take the problem to the person who gave him the assignment
   D. say nothing to anyone about his complaint

In answering this question, you should study each of the choices to find which is best. Consider choice "A" – Certainly an employee may discuss his complaint with fellow employees, but no change or improvement can result, and the complaint remains unresolved. Choice "B" is a poor choice since the head of the organization probably does not know what assignment you have been given, and taking your problem to him is known as "going over the head" of the supervisor. The supervisor, or person who made the assignment, is the person who can clarify it or correct any injustice. Choice "C" is, therefore, correct. To say nothing, as in choice "D," is unwise. Supervisors have and interest in knowing the problems employees are facing, and the employee is seeking a solution to his problem.

2) True/False Questions

The "true/false" or "right/wrong" form of question is sometimes used. Here a complete statement is given. Your job is to decide whether the statement is right or wrong.

SAMPLE: A roaming cell-phone call to a nearby city costs less than a non-roaming call to a distant city.

This statement is wrong, or false, since roaming calls are more expensive.

This is not a complete list of all possible question forms, although most of the others are variations of these common types. You will always get complete directions for answering questions. Be sure you understand *how* to mark your answers – ask questions until you do.

V. RECORDING YOUR ANSWERS

Computer terminals are used more and more today for many different kinds of exams.

For an examination with very few applicants, you may be told to record your answers in the test booklet itself. Separate answer sheets are much more common. If this separate answer sheet is to be scored by machine – and this is often the case – it is highly important that you mark your answers correctly in order to get credit.

An electronic scoring machine is often used in civil service offices because of the speed with which papers can be scored. Machine-scored answer sheets must be marked with a pencil, which will be given to you. This pencil has a high graphite content which responds to the electronic scoring machine. As a matter of fact, stray dots may register as answers, so do not let your pencil rest on the answer sheet while you are pondering the correct answer. Also, if your pencil lead breaks or is otherwise defective, ask for another.

Since the answer sheet will be dropped in a slot in the scoring machine, be careful not to bend the corners or get the paper crumpled.

The answer sheet normally has five vertical columns of numbers, with 30 numbers to a column. These numbers correspond to the question numbers in your test booklet. After each number, going across the page are four or five pairs of dotted lines. These short dotted lines have small letters or numbers above them. The first two pairs may also have a "T" or "F" above the letters. This indicates that the first two pairs only are to be used if the questions are of the true-false type. If the questions are multiple choice, disregard the "T" and "F" and pay attention only to the small letters or numbers.

Answer your questions in the manner of the sample that follows:

32. The largest city in the United States is
    A. Washington, D.C.
    B. New York City
    C. Chicago
    D. Detroit
    E. San Francisco

1) Choose the answer you think is best. (New York City is the largest, so "B" is correct.)
2) Find the row of dotted lines numbered the same as the question you are answering. (Find row number 32)
3) Find the pair of dotted lines corresponding to the answer. (Find the pair of lines under the mark "B.")
4) Make a solid black mark between the dotted lines.

VI. BEFORE THE TEST

Common sense will help you find procedures to follow to get ready for an examination. Too many of us, however, overlook these sensible measures. Indeed, nervousness and fatigue have been found to be the most serious reasons why applicants fail to do their best on civil service tests. Here is a list of reminders:

- Begin your preparation early – Don't wait until the last minute to go scurrying around for books and materials or to find out what the position is all about.
- Prepare continuously – An hour a night for a week is better than an all-night cram session. This has been definitely established. What is more, a night a week for a month will return better dividends than crowding your study into a shorter period of time.
- Locate the place of the exam – You have been sent a notice telling you when and where to report for the examination. If the location is in a different town or otherwise unfamiliar to you, it would be well to inquire the best route and learn something about the building.
- Relax the night before the test – Allow your mind to rest. Do not study at all that night. Plan some mild recreation or diversion; then go to bed early and get a good night's sleep.
- Get up early enough to make a leisurely trip to the place for the test – This way unforeseen events, traffic snarls, unfamiliar buildings, etc. will not upset you.
- Dress comfortably – A written test is not a fashion show. You will be known by number and not by name, so wear something comfortable.

- Leave excess paraphernalia at home – Shopping bags and odd bundles will get in your way. You need bring only the items mentioned in the official notice you received; usually everything you need is provided. Do not bring reference books to the exam. They will only confuse those last minutes and be taken away from you when in the test room.
- Arrive somewhat ahead of time – If because of transportation schedules you must get there very early, bring a newspaper or magazine to take your mind off yourself while waiting.
- Locate the examination room – When you have found the proper room, you will be directed to the seat or part of the room where you will sit. Sometimes you are given a sheet of instructions to read while you are waiting. Do not fill out any forms until you are told to do so; just read them and be prepared.
- Relax and prepare to listen to the instructions
- If you have any physical problem that may keep you from doing your best, be sure to tell the test administrator. If you are sick or in poor health, you really cannot do your best on the exam. You can come back and take the test some other time.

VII. AT THE TEST

The day of the test is here and you have the test booklet in your hand. The temptation to get going is very strong. Caution! There is more to success than knowing the right answers. You must know how to identify your papers and understand variations in the type of short-answer question used in this particular examination. Follow these suggestions for maximum results from your efforts:

1) Cooperate with the monitor

The test administrator has a duty to create a situation in which you can be as much at ease as possible. He will give instructions, tell you when to begin, check to see that you are marking your answer sheet correctly, and so on. He is not there to guard you, although he will see that your competitors do not take unfair advantage. He wants to help you do your best.

2) Listen to all instructions

Don't jump the gun! Wait until you understand all directions. In most civil service tests you get more time than you need to answer the questions. So don't be in a hurry. Read each word of instructions until you clearly understand the meaning. Study the examples, listen to all announcements and follow directions. Ask questions if you do not understand what to do.

3) Identify your papers

Civil service exams are usually identified by number only. You will be assigned a number; you must not put your name on your test papers. Be sure to copy your number correctly. Since more than one exam may be given, copy your exact examination title.

4) Plan your time

Unless you are told that a test is a "speed" or "rate of work" test, speed itself is usually not important. Time enough to answer all the questions will be provided, but this does not mean that you have all day. An overall time limit has been set. Divide the total time (in minutes) by the number of questions to determine the approximate time you have for each question.

5) Do not linger over difficult questions

If you come across a difficult question, mark it with a paper clip (useful to have along) and come back to it when you have been through the booklet. One caution if you do this – be sure to skip a number on your answer sheet as well. Check often to be sure that you have not lost your place and that you are marking in the row numbered the same as the question you are answering.

6) Read the questions

Be sure you know what the question asks! Many capable people are unsuccessful because they failed to *read* the questions correctly.

7) Answer all questions

Unless you have been instructed that a penalty will be deducted for incorrect answers, it is better to guess than to omit a question.

8) Speed tests

It is often better NOT to guess on speed tests. It has been found that on timed tests people are tempted to spend the last few seconds before time is called in marking answers at random – without even reading them – in the hope of picking up a few extra points. To discourage this practice, the instructions may warn you that your score will be "corrected" for guessing. That is, a penalty will be applied. The incorrect answers will be deducted from the correct ones, or some other penalty formula will be used.

9) Review your answers

If you finish before time is called, go back to the questions you guessed or omitted to give them further thought. Review other answers if you have time.

10) Return your test materials

If you are ready to leave before others have finished or time is called, take ALL your materials to the monitor and leave quietly. Never take any test material with you. The monitor can discover whose papers are not complete, and taking a test booklet may be grounds for disqualification.

VIII. EXAMINATION TECHNIQUES

1) Read the general instructions carefully. These are usually printed on the first page of the exam booklet. As a rule, these instructions refer to the timing of the examination; the fact that you should not start work until the signal and must stop work at a signal, etc. If there are any *special* instructions, such as a choice of questions to be answered, make sure that you note this instruction carefully.

2) When you are ready to start work on the examination, that is as soon as the signal has been given, read the instructions to each question booklet, underline any key words or phrases, such as *least, best, outline, describe* and the like. In this way you will tend to answer as requested rather than discover on reviewing your paper that you *listed without describing*, that you selected the *worst* choice rather than the *best* choice, etc.

3) If the examination is of the objective or multiple-choice type – that is, each question will also give a series of possible answers: A, B, C or D, and you are called upon to select the best answer and write the letter next to that answer on your answer paper – it is advisable to start answering each question in turn. There may be anywhere from 50 to 100 such questions in the three or four hours allotted and you can see how much time would be taken if you read through all the questions before beginning to answer any. Furthermore, if you come across a question or group of questions which you know would be difficult to answer, it would undoubtedly affect your handling of all the other questions.

4) If the examination is of the essay type and contains but a few questions, it is a moot point as to whether you should read all the questions before starting to answer any one. Of course, if you are given a choice – say five out of seven and the like – then it is essential to read all the questions so you can eliminate the two that are most difficult. If, however, you are asked to answer all the questions, there may be danger in trying to answer the easiest one first because you may find that you will spend too much time on it. The best technique is to answer the first question, then proceed to the second, etc.

5) Time your answers. Before the exam begins, write down the time it started, then add the time allowed for the examination and write down the time it must be completed, then divide the time available somewhat as follows:
    - If 3-1/2 hours are allowed, that would be 210 minutes. If you have 80 objective-type questions, that would be an average of 2-1/2 minutes per question. Allow yourself no more than 2 minutes per question, or a total of 160 minutes, which will permit about 50 minutes to review.
    - If for the time allotment of 210 minutes there are 7 essay questions to answer, that would average about 30 minutes a question. Give yourself only 25 minutes per question so that you have about 35 minutes to review.

6) The most important instruction is to *read each question* and make sure you know what is wanted. The second most important instruction is to *time yourself properly* so that you answer every question. The third most important instruction is to *answer every question*. Guess if you have to but include something for each question. Remember that you will receive no credit for a blank and will probably receive some credit if you write something in answer to an essay question. If you guess a letter – say "B" for a multiple-choice question – you may have guessed right. If you leave a blank as an answer to a multiple-choice question, the examiners may respect your feelings but it will not add a point to your score. Some exams may penalize you for wrong answers, so in such cases *only*, you may not want to guess unless you have some basis for your answer.

7) Suggestions
    a. Objective-type questions
        1. Examine the question booklet for proper sequence of pages and questions
        2. Read all instructions carefully
        3. Skip any question which seems too difficult; return to it after all other questions have been answered
        4. Apportion your time properly; do not spend too much time on any single question or group of questions

5. Note and underline key words – *all, most, fewest, least, best, worst, same, opposite*, etc.
6. Pay particular attention to negatives
7. Note unusual option, e.g., unduly long, short, complex, different or similar in content to the body of the question
8. Observe the use of "hedging" words – *probably, may, most likely*, etc.
9. Make sure that your answer is put next to the same number as the question
10. Do not second-guess unless you have good reason to believe the second answer is definitely more correct
11. Cross out original answer if you decide another answer is more accurate; do not erase until you are ready to hand your paper in
12. Answer all questions; guess unless instructed otherwise
13. Leave time for review

b. Essay questions
1. Read each question carefully
2. Determine exactly what is wanted. Underline key words or phrases.
3. Decide on outline or paragraph answer
4. Include many different points and elements unless asked to develop any one or two points or elements
5. Show impartiality by giving pros and cons unless directed to select one side only
6. Make and write down any assumptions you find necessary to answer the questions
7. Watch your English, grammar, punctuation and choice of words
8. Time your answers; don't crowd material

8) Answering the essay question

Most essay questions can be answered by framing the specific response around several key words or ideas. Here are a few such key words or ideas:

M's: manpower, materials, methods, money, management
P's: purpose, program, policy, plan, procedure, practice, problems, pitfalls, personnel, public relations

a. Six basic steps in handling problems:
1. Preliminary plan and background development
2. Collect information, data and facts
3. Analyze and interpret information, data and facts
4. Analyze and develop solutions as well as make recommendations
5. Prepare report and sell recommendations
6. Install recommendations and follow up effectiveness

b. Pitfalls to avoid
1. *Taking things for granted* – A statement of the situation does not necessarily imply that each of the elements is necessarily true; for example, a complaint may be invalid and biased so that all that can be taken for granted is that a complaint has been registered

2. *Considering only one side of a situation* – Wherever possible, indicate several alternatives and then point out the reasons you selected the best one
3. *Failing to indicate follow up* – Whenever your answer indicates action on your part, make certain that you will take proper follow-up action to see how successful your recommendations, procedures or actions turn out to be
4. *Taking too long in answering any single question* – Remember to time your answers properly

IX. AFTER THE TEST

Scoring procedures differ in detail among civil service jurisdictions although the general principles are the same. Whether the papers are hand-scored or graded by machine we have described, they are nearly always graded by number. That is, the person who marks the paper knows only the number – never the name – of the applicant. Not until all the papers have been graded will they be matched with names. If other tests, such as training and experience or oral interview ratings have been given, scores will be combined. Different parts of the examination usually have different weights. For example, the written test might count 60 percent of the final grade, and a rating of training and experience 40 percent. In many jurisdictions, veterans will have a certain number of points added to their grades.

After the final grade has been determined, the names are placed in grade order and an eligible list is established. There are various methods for resolving ties between those who get the same final grade – probably the most common is to place first the name of the person whose application was received first. Job offers are made from the eligible list in the order the names appear on it. You will be notified of your grade and your rank as soon as all these computations have been made. This will be done as rapidly as possible.

People who are found to meet the requirements in the announcement are called "eligibles." Their names are put on a list of eligible candidates. An eligible's chances of getting a job depend on how high he stands on this list and how fast agencies are filling jobs from the list.

When a job is to be filled from a list of eligibles, the agency asks for the names of people on the list of eligibles for that job. When the civil service commission receives this request, it sends to the agency the names of the three people highest on this list. Or, if the job to be filled has specialized requirements, the office sends the agency the names of the top three persons who meet these requirements from the general list.

The appointing officer makes a choice from among the three people whose names were sent to him. If the selected person accepts the appointment, the names of the others are put back on the list to be considered for future openings.

That is the rule in hiring from all kinds of eligible lists, whether they are for typist, carpenter, chemist, or something else. For every vacancy, the appointing officer has his choice of any one of the top three eligibles on the list. This explains why the person whose name is on top of the list sometimes does not get an appointment when some of the persons lower on the list do. If the appointing officer chooses the second or third eligible, the No. 1 eligible does not get a job at once, but stays on the list until he is appointed or the list is terminated.

X. HOW TO PASS THE INTERVIEW TEST

The examination for which you applied requires an oral interview test. You have already taken the written test and you are now being called for the interview test – the final part of the formal examination.

You may think that it is not possible to prepare for an interview test and that there are no procedures to follow during an interview. Our purpose is to point out some things you can do in advance that will help you and some good rules to follow and pitfalls to avoid while you are being interviewed.

What is an interview supposed to test?

The written examination is designed to test the technical knowledge and competence of the candidate; the oral is designed to evaluate intangible qualities, not readily measured otherwise, and to establish a list showing the relative fitness of each candidate – as measured against his competitors – for the position sought. Scoring is not on the basis of "right" and "wrong," but on a sliding scale of values ranging from "not passable" to "outstanding." As a matter of fact, it is possible to achieve a relatively low score without a single "incorrect" answer because of evident weakness in the qualities being measured.

Occasionally, an examination may consist entirely of an oral test – either an individual or a group oral. In such cases, information is sought concerning the technical knowledges and abilities of the candidate, since there has been no written examination for this purpose. More commonly, however, an oral test is used to supplement a written examination.

Who conducts interviews?

The composition of oral boards varies among different jurisdictions. In nearly all, a representative of the personnel department serves as chairman. One of the members of the board may be a representative of the department in which the candidate would work. In some cases, "outside experts" are used, and, frequently, a businessman or some other representative of the general public is asked to serve. Labor and management or other special groups may be represented. The aim is to secure the services of experts in the appropriate field.

However the board is composed, it is a good idea (and not at all improper or unethical) to ascertain in advance of the interview who the members are and what groups they represent. When you are introduced to them, you will have some idea of their backgrounds and interests, and at least you will not stutter and stammer over their names.

What should be done before the interview?

While knowledge about the board members is useful and takes some of the surprise element out of the interview, there is other preparation which is more substantive. It *is* possible to prepare for an oral interview – in several ways:

1) Keep a copy of your application and review it carefully before the interview

This may be the only document before the oral board, and the starting point of the interview. Know what education and experience you have listed there, and the sequence and dates of all of it. Sometimes the board will ask you to review the highlights of your experience for them; you should not have to hem and haw doing it.

2) Study the class specification and the examination announcement

Usually, the oral board has one or both of these to guide them. The qualities, characteristics or knowledges required by the position sought are stated in these documents. They offer valuable clues as to the nature of the oral interview. For example, if the job involves supervisory responsibilities, the announcement will usually indicate that knowledge of modern supervisory methods and the qualifications of the candidate as a supervisor will be tested. If so, you can expect such questions, frequently in the form of a hypothetical situation which you are expected to solve. NEVER go into an oral without knowledge of the duties and responsibilities of the job you seek.

3) Think through each qualification required

Try to visualize the kind of questions you would ask if you were a board member. How well could you answer them? Try especially to appraise your own knowledge and background in each area, *measured against the job sought*, and identify any areas in which you are weak. Be critical and realistic – do not flatter yourself.

4) Do some general reading in areas in which you feel you may be weak

For example, if the job involves supervision and your past experience has NOT, some general reading in supervisory methods and practices, particularly in the field of human relations, might be useful. Do NOT study agency procedures or detailed manuals. The oral board will be testing your understanding and capacity, not your memory.

5) Get a good night's sleep and watch your general health and mental attitude

You will want a clear head at the interview. Take care of a cold or any other minor ailment, and of course, no hangovers.

What should be done on the day of the interview?

Now comes the day of the interview itself. Give yourself plenty of time to get there. Plan to arrive somewhat ahead of the scheduled time, particularly if your appointment is in the fore part of the day. If a previous candidate fails to appear, the board might be ready for you a bit early. By early afternoon an oral board is almost invariably behind schedule if there are many candidates, and you may have to wait. Take along a book or magazine to read, or your application to review, but leave any extraneous material in the waiting room when you go in for your interview. In any event, relax and compose yourself.

The matter of dress is important. The board is forming impressions about you – from your experience, your manners, your attitude, and your appearance. Give your personal appearance careful attention. Dress your best, but not your flashiest. Choose conservative, appropriate clothing, and be sure it is immaculate. This is a business interview, and your appearance should indicate that you regard it as such. Besides, being well groomed and properly dressed will help boost your confidence.

Sooner or later, someone will call your name and escort you into the interview room. *This is it.* From here on you are on your own. It is too late for any more preparation. But remember, you asked for this opportunity to prove your fitness, and you are here because your request was granted.

What happens when you go in?

The usual sequence of events will be as follows: The clerk (who is often the board stenographer) will introduce you to the chairman of the oral board, who will introduce you to the other members of the board. Acknowledge the introductions before you sit down. Do not be surprised if you find a microphone facing you or a stenotypist sitting by. Oral interviews are usually recorded in the event of an appeal or other review.

Usually the chairman of the board will open the interview by reviewing the highlights of your education and work experience from your application – primarily for the benefit of the other members of the board, as well as to get the material into the record. Do not interrupt or comment unless there is an error or significant misinterpretation; if that is the case, do not hesitate. But do not quibble about insignificant matters. Also, he will usually ask you some question about your education, experience or your present job – partly to get you to start talking and to establish the interviewing "rapport." He may start the actual questioning, or turn it over to one of the other members. Frequently, each member undertakes the questioning on a particular area, one in which he is perhaps most competent, so you can expect each member to participate in the examination. Because time is limited, you may also expect some rather abrupt switches in the direction the questioning takes, so do not be upset by it. Normally, a board member will not pursue a single line of questioning unless he discovers a particular strength or weakness.

After each member has participated, the chairman will usually ask whether any member has any further questions, then will ask you if you have anything you wish to add. Unless you are expecting this question, it may floor you. Worse, it may start you off on an extended, extemporaneous speech. The board is not usually seeking more information. The question is principally to offer you a last opportunity to present further qualifications or to indicate that you have nothing to add. So, if you feel that a significant qualification or characteristic has been overlooked, it is proper to point it out in a sentence or so. Do not compliment the board on the thoroughness of their examination – they have been sketchy, and you know it. If you wish, merely say, "No thank you, I have nothing further to add." This is a point where you can "talk yourself out" of a good impression or fail to present an important bit of information. Remember, *you close the interview yourself*.

The chairman will then say, "That is all, Mr. _____, thank you." Do not be startled; the interview is over, and quicker than you think. Thank him, gather your belongings and take your leave. Save your sigh of relief for the other side of the door.

How to put your best foot forward

Throughout this entire process, you may feel that the board individually and collectively is trying to pierce your defenses, seek out your hidden weaknesses and embarrass and confuse you. Actually, this is not true. They are obliged to make an appraisal of your qualifications for the job you are seeking, and they want to see you in your best light. Remember, they must interview all candidates and a non-cooperative candidate may become a failure in spite of their best efforts to bring out his qualifications. Here are 15 suggestions that will help you:

1) Be natural – Keep your attitude confident, not cocky

If you are not confident that you can do the job, do not expect the board to be. Do not apologize for your weaknesses, try to bring out your strong points. The board is interested in a positive, not negative, presentation. Cockiness will antagonize any board member and make him wonder if you are covering up a weakness by a false show of strength.

2) Get comfortable, but don't lounge or sprawl

Sit erectly but not stiffly. A careless posture may lead the board to conclude that you are careless in other things, or at least that you are not impressed by the importance of the occasion. Either conclusion is natural, even if incorrect. Do not fuss with your clothing, a pencil or an ashtray. Your hands may occasionally be useful to emphasize a point; do not let them become a point of distraction.

3) Do not wisecrack or make small talk

This is a serious situation, and your attitude should show that you consider it as such. Further, the time of the board is limited – they do not want to waste it, and neither should you.

4) Do not exaggerate your experience or abilities

In the first place, from information in the application or other interviews and sources, the board may know more about you than you think. Secondly, you probably will not get away with it. An experienced board is rather adept at spotting such a situation, so do not take the chance.

5) If you know a board member, do not make a point of it, yet do not hide it

Certainly you are not fooling him, and probably not the other members of the board. Do not try to take advantage of your acquaintanceship – it will probably do you little good.

6) Do not dominate the interview

Let the board do that. They will give you the clues – do not assume that you have to do all the talking. Realize that the board has a number of questions to ask you, and do not try to take up all the interview time by showing off your extensive knowledge of the answer to the first one.

7) Be attentive

You only have 20 minutes or so, and you should keep your attention at its sharpest throughout. When a member is addressing a problem or question to you, give him your undivided attention. Address your reply principally to him, but do not exclude the other board members.

8) Do not interrupt

A board member may be stating a problem for you to analyze. He will ask you a question when the time comes. Let him state the problem, and wait for the question.

9) Make sure you understand the question

Do not try to answer until you are sure what the question is. If it is not clear, restate it in your own words or ask the board member to clarify it for you. However, do not haggle about minor elements.

10) Reply promptly but not hastily

A common entry on oral board rating sheets is "candidate responded readily," or "candidate hesitated in replies." Respond as promptly and quickly as you can, but do not jump to a hasty, ill-considered answer.

11) Do not be peremptory in your answers

A brief answer is proper – but do not fire your answer back. That is a losing game from your point of view. The board member can probably ask questions much faster than you can answer them.

12) Do not try to create the answer you think the board member wants

He is interested in what kind of mind you have and how it works – not in playing games. Furthermore, he can usually spot this practice and will actually grade you down on it.

13) Do not switch sides in your reply merely to agree with a board member

Frequently, a member will take a contrary position merely to draw you out and to see if you are willing and able to defend your point of view. Do not start a debate, yet do not surrender a good position. If a position is worth taking, it is worth defending.

14) Do not be afraid to admit an error in judgment if you are shown to be wrong

The board knows that you are forced to reply without any opportunity for careful consideration. Your answer may be demonstrably wrong. If so, admit it and get on with the interview.

15) Do not dwell at length on your present job

The opening question may relate to your present assignment. Answer the question but do not go into an extended discussion. You are being examined for a *new* job, not your present one. As a matter of fact, try to phrase ALL your answers in terms of the job for which you are being examined.

Basis of Rating

Probably you will forget most of these "do's" and "don'ts" when you walk into the oral interview room. Even remembering them all will not ensure you a passing grade. Perhaps you did not have the qualifications in the first place. But remembering them will help you to put your best foot forward, without treading on the toes of the board members.

Rumor and popular opinion to the contrary notwithstanding, an oral board wants you to make the best appearance possible. They know you are under pressure – but they also want to see how you respond to it as a guide to what your reaction would be under the pressures of the job you seek. They will be influenced by the degree of poise you display, the personal traits you show and the manner in which you respond.

ABOUT THIS BOOK

This book contains tests divided into Examination Sections. Go through each test, answering every question in the margin. We have also attached a sample answer sheet at the back of the book that can be removed and used. At the end of each test look at the answer key and check your answers. On the ones you got wrong, look at the right answer choice and learn. Do not fill in the answers first. Do not memorize the questions and answers, but understand the answer and principles involved. On your test, the questions will likely be different from the samples. Questions are changed and new ones added. If you understand these past questions you should have success with any changes that arise. Tests may consist of several types of questions. We have additional books on each subject should more study be advisable or necessary for you. Finally, the more you study, the better prepared you will be. This book is intended to be the last thing you study before you walk into the examination room. Prior study of relevant texts is also recommended. NLC publishes some of these in our Fundamental Series. Knowledge and good sense are important factors in passing your exam. Good luck also helps. So now study this Passbook, absorb the material contained within and take that knowledge into the examination. Then do your best to pass that exam.

EXAMINATION SECTION

EXAMINATION SECTION
TEST 1

DIRECTIONS: Each question or incomplete statement is followed by several suggested answers or completions. Select the one that *BEST* answers the question or completes the statement. *PRINT THE LETTER OF THE CORRECT ANSWER IN THE SPACE AT THE RIGHT.*

1. It has been stated that in renting there is no substitute for accompanying a prospect to the space you are trying to rent. Of the following, the MOST important reason for this is that

    A. prospects are not likely to be willing to inspect space unless they are accompanied
    B. prospects are likely to see the least attractive points of the available space unless skillfully diverted from them
    C. the real estate manager is able to exhibit the good points of the space
    D. the presence of the real estate manager alerts the staff to the necessity for making a good impression

    1._____

2. As real estate manager, you have commercial space for rent which contains a certain defect which is known to you. In showing the space to a prospective tenant it would be *ADVISABLE tor* you to

    A. attempt to ignore the defect and disparage its importance if it is mentioned by the prospect
    B. explain the defect in advance of showing the space to the prospect
    C. ignore the defect and immediately change the subject if it is mentioned by the prospect
    D. show the space at a time when the defect may not be apparent

    2._____

3. The owner of a building containing commercial space has informed his renting agent of the rent he expects to receive for this commercial space. When shown the space and told of the rent, a prospective tenant, of good reputation, agrees immediately and without argument to rent the space. It would be *BEST* for the renting agent to

    A. indicate that he has made an error and ask for a somewhat higher rent which the prospect may be willing to pay
    B. make immediate arrangements to close the deal on the basis of the rent already discussed
    C. set conditions of leasing, other than rent, which are disadvantageous to the prospect, indicating that these conditions may be withdrawn if a higher rent is agreed upon
    D. make no binding commitment until he has an opportunity to look for other prospective tenants who might be willing to pay a higher rental

    3._____

4. Assume that approximately 7% of the commercial rental space in a neighborhood is vacant and that this and other rental conditions are the same now as they were when certain commercial space, for which you are managing agent, was last rented. The lease is about to expire on the commercial space. Faced with the problem of renting the space to a new tenant or renewing the occupancy of the present tenant, it is *USUALLY* true that

    4._____

A. new tenants are willing to pay higher rents than old tenants
B. new tenants make fewer demands than old tenants if the real estate agent is of good reputation
C. old tenants make fewer demands than new tenants if the real estate agent has properly handled their requests while under the old lease
D. it is more desirable to get a new tenant than retain an old one

5. The one of the following factors to which you should give LEAST consideration in determining the rental value of office space in a building under your management is

    A. accessibility of the building to means of transportation
    B. height of the ceilings in the office space
    C. prestige value of tenancy in the building
    D. rental value of office space in other buildings in the neighborhood

6. The LEAST accurate of the following statements concerning the determination of the rental value of office space within an office building is:

    A. Space along the side of the building is less valuable than space on a corner.
    B. The better the view from windows in the space, the more valuable is the space.
    C. Above the eighth floor, the higher the floor, the less valuable the space.
    D. The more accessible space is to the toilet facilities (of modern design), the more valuable it is.

7. One of the factors to be considered in renting apartments is the likelihood that the prospective tenant may later wish to renew his lease. In a building in a stable neighborhood, the one of the following types of families which a real estate manager should LEAST expect to want to remain after the expiration of the lease is a

    A. single person, age about 67 years
    B. young couple, age about 25 years
    C. couple, age about 40 years, with two children, age 7 and 9 years
    D. couple, age about 45 years, with four children age 7, 8, 9 and 12 years

8. Assume that a great deal of building is going on in a neighborhood where there is much unimproved land in order to take care of an increasing population. It is to be expected that real estate values in this neighborhood are

    A. decreasing
    B. increasing
    C. increasing for existing buildings while decreasing for unimproved land
    D. remaining relatively constant

9. In a neighborhood where there is a trend toward increasing population due to conversions of private dwellings into rooming houses, the value of neighborhood real estate will generally be

    A. decreasing
    B. increasing
    C. increasing for unimproved land but decreasing for land having residential buildings
    D. unaffected

10. An apartment consists of the following: a living room 12 ft. X 14 ft.; a bedroom 8 ft. X 8 ft.; a bathroom 6 ft. X 6 ft.; a bedroom 11 ft. X 12 ft.; a kitchen 6 ft. X 10 ft., at one end of which is a dining area 6 ft. X 6 ft. separated from the kitchen by room dividers in the form of 5 ft. high cabinets; a hallway 4 ft. X 15 ft.; two closets 2 1/2 ft. X 5 ft.; and a closet 4 ft. X 7 ft. The only windows in the apartment are in the bedrooms, living room, kitchen, and bathroom. According to the system of calculation generally used, the number of rooms in this apartment is

    A. 3 1/2 B. 4 1/2 C. 4 3/4 D. 5 1/4

11. The one of the following statements which is NOT a valid reason for demanding a security deposit of a month's rent as part of the lease agreement is:

    A. Ability to pay a security deposit as well as the first month's rent before taking occupancy tends to indicate that a tenant is solvent.
    B. Current expenses of the building may in part be defrayed by security deposits.
    C. If a tenant moves before the expiration of his lease, the security deposit reduces the loss due to vacancy that is likely to occur.
    D. Loss of income will be minimized in the event that action to evict a tenant for non-payment of rent becomes necessary.

12. At the expiration of a lease on commercial space where the tenant has installed sinks and toilets, it is the USUAL practice that ownership of these fixtures

    A. passes to the landlord
    B. passes to the landlord, with the tenant retaining the right of purchase at a price equal to the original cost less depreciation
    C. remains with the tenant
    D. remains with the tenant, unless otherwise specified in the lease

13. The term "percentage lease," when used in connection with leasing of a store, refers USUALLY to an agreement

    A. to assume the remaining portion of an existing lease and at its termination to renew the lease at an agreed percentage increase
    B. to lease a percentage portion of previously undivided premises and to erect suitable partitions
    C. to pay a fixed rent plus a percentage of the tenant's gross receipts above an agreed amount
    D. among several lessees of one premises, each to assume responsibility for a percentage portion of an undivided premises and a percentage portion of the lease

14. The term "title insurance" refers to insurance that protects a

    A. prospective purchaser with a preliminary purchase agreement against refusal of the owner to convey title of the property
    B. purchaser against any outstanding taxes or liens against the property prior to the transfer of title
    C. purchaser against damage to property between the time of the agreement to purchase and the final transfer of title
    D. purchaser against the discovery of a defect in the seller's title to the property

15. Where a store or commercial establishment which uses water is situated in a residential building, the MAJORITY of commercial lease agreements provide that

   A. a fixed amount be paid with the rent to the landlord to cover water use
   B. a fixed percentage of the water charge for the building be paid by the commercial tenant
   C. water charges be paid by the landlord
   D. water charges, dependent upon water use, be paid separately by the commercial tenant

16. The LEAST amount of time that it will take to have a tenant removed from an apartment for non-payment of rent, from the date that the owner decides to evict the tenant, who is already more than one month delinquent in the payment of his rent, is GENERALLY

   A. less than 7 days
   B. between 13 and 19 days
   C. between 17 and 30 days
   D. not less than 10 months

17. The one of the following which is NOT provided for by Workmen's Compensation Insurance is payment

   A. for hospitalization of the injured employee
   B. for medicines and crutches or other implements that may be necessary to restore the employee's health
   C. when an injury is due to the employee's being under the influence of alcohol
   D. when an injury is due to the employee's own negligence

18. Public liability insurance GENERALLY protects the insured, landlord when

   A. a tenant's property is damaged by water used to put out a fire in another tenant's apartment
   B. a visitor to one of the tenants is injured by falling over a worn and broken step at the entrance to the building
   C. an employee is injured while performing his assigned duties
   D. damage to the building has been caused by an airplane crash

19. Assuming that sufficient fire insurance is carried, the MOST important factor considered by fire insurance companies in making a settlement after a fire has destroyed a building is the _____ of the building.

   A. assessed valuation
   B. most recent sale price
   C. original construction cost
   D. replacement cost

20. In purchasing fire insurance in your State, it should be realized that

   A. all members of the Board of Fire Underwriters will charge the same rates, while non-member companies may have different rates
   B. insurance companies incorporated in your State all charge the rates which are fixed by law, while out-of-state companies are free to charge any rates that they deem appropriate
   C. insurance rates are determined by bargaining between the insurance broker and the prospective customer as in any free market
   D. no rate agreements exist, each insurance company individually determining its own rates based upon such factors as past experience, profit margins, and competitive position

21. The owner of a building in a city of over one million population proposes to carry one percent co-insurance to protect himself against loss by fire. It would generally be *BEST* for a real estate agent to recommend that

    A. a greater amount of insurance be purchased if the replacement cost of the building is greater than the original construction cost
    B. a lesser amount be purchased because total loss of a building in this city by fire is unlikely
    C. a lesser amount be purchased since insurance companies will not sell insurance for the full value of a building
    D. the insurance be purchased if the owner has the funds available to pay the premiums

22. From the point of view of good real estate management, a tenant should *FIRST be* told of the necessity to pay his rent on time

    A. when he makes application for a lease
    B. whenever he is more than one week delinquent in the payment of his rent
    C. whenever he is more than three days delinquent in the payment of his rent
    D. within the first month after the lease becomes operative

23. If a tenant refuses to pay his rent until the real estate manager has had an inexpensive but necessary repair made, it would be *BEST* for the real estate manager to

    A. refuse even to consider the repair until the rent is paid
    B. explain to the tenant that he has an obligation to pay rent but agree to investigate the need for the repair, insisting that rent be paid after the investigation is completed
    C. have the repair made and then insist on the payment of rent
    D. insist that the rent be paid, refusing to couple consideration of the need for the repair with the payment of rent

24. Examination of the public hallways of a building containing tile floors reveals that a blackened and dirty area exists along the base of the walls, extending up the walls for a couple of inches. The *MOST* likely of the following explanations for this condition is that

    A. children have been scuffing their feet along the walls
    B. it is a normal development caused by the traffic of dirty feet in the halls, elimination of the dirty area being impractical because of the expense
    C. the floors have been cleaned with a mop which was not sufficiently clean
    D. there is a structural fault in the flooring or walls requiring immediate attention from an expert

25. The charge for water supplied by cities of over one million population to an apartment house with no commercial tenants is *GENERALLY* made on the basis of

    A. assessed valuation of the building
    B. frontage and number of apartments
    C. frontage, number of stories, and number and type of water outlets
    D. water meter readings

KEY (CORRECT ANSWERS)

1.	C	11.	B
2.	B	12.	A
3.	B	13.	C
4.	C	14.	D
5.	B	15.	D
6.	C	16.	B
7.	B	17.	C
8.	B	18.	B
9.	A	19.	D
10.	B	20.	A

21. B
22. A
23. D
24. C
25. C

TEST 2

DIRECTIONS: Each question or incomplete statement is followed by several suggested answers or completions. Select the one that *BEST* answers the question or completes the statement. *PRINT THE LETTER OF THE CORRECT ANSWER IN THE SPACE AT THE RIGHT.*

1. The term HATCH DOOR is generally used to describe a door 1.____

    A. between the outdoors and the basement
    B. giving access from the boiler room to the fire tubes of a boiler
    C. giving access to the roof from the top of the stairway
    D. giving entrance from the hallway to the elevator shaft

2. A *PARAPET* is 2.____

    A. a device through which a fine spray of oil enters the firebox of an oil burner
    B. a hot water drain used mornings to bleed off cold water which has accumulated overnight
    C. a protective low wall at the edge of a roof
    D. the primary support of an arch

3. *2-4-D is* used to designate 3.____

    A. an oil moisture used to start an oil burner in operation
    B. a size of threaded pipe of the type used to carry waste water
    C. a type of weed killer for use on lawns
    D. a type of pre-mixed cement for patching walks

4. A *CONDENSER* is a part of a 4.____

    A. boiler where the oil is preheated
    B. fertilizer spreader where concentrated fertilizer is mixed with water
    C. radiator where the return water forms from steam
    D. refrigerator where the refrigerant takes liquid form

5. A *LOW WATER CUT-OFF* is usually a device to 5.____

    A. close the waste line opening when the waste has flushed out of the toilet bowl
    B. shut down the automatic lawn-watering system when the moisture level in the lawn reaches a predetermined level of saturation
    C. stop a sump pump when the water level is below floor level in the sump well
    D. stop an oil burner motor when the water level in the system falls below a predetermined level

6. The purpose of a *CHECK VALVE* is to 6.____

    A. interrupt the flow of electricity in an overloaded circuit
    B. limit the amount of electrical current which can fl flow from a main line into a branch circuit
    C. prevent water from flowing in a pipe system in a direction opposite to that desired
    D. stop the flow of water when the water in a system reaches a predetermined level

7. An investigation has been made of a broken window pane in an apartment on the third floor which the tenant claims was broken by children playing outside. The investigation disclosed that there were several small holes in the window pane. Each hole is approximately cone shaped and is about 3/16 inch in diameter on the inside of the glass (room side) and about 1/2 inch in diameter on the outside. Cracks connected some of these holes. On the basis of this information, the tenant should

    A. be charged for the window pane since the damage is not normal wear and tear and it is not possible to substantiate the tenant's claim
    B. be charged for the window pane since the nature of the damage indicates that it was caused from inside
    C. not be charged for the window pane since it is not possible to determine the cause of the damage and the low floor involved does not tend to support the tenant's explanation
    D. not be charged for the window pane since the nature of the damage indicates that it was caused from outside

8. The one of the following which has come into common use for the extermination of roaches and silverfish is

    A. 2-4 D   B. chlordane   C. paris green   D. red squill

9. When the building superintendent tells you that the transformer of one of the oil burners is defective, he is referring to the device which

    A. atomizes the liquid oil prior to ignition
    B. changes low pressure steam to high pressure steam
    C. increases the voltage for oil ignition
    D. regulates oil temperature prior to atomization

10. When a building superintendent reports corroded flashings resulting in leakage, the part of the building he is referring to is the

    A. basement piping   B. boiler room
    C. pavement adjoining building D. roof

11. If an automatic elevator is not leveling properly at floor stops, the proper action to take is to

    A. allow the car to remain in service only if the distance between the car floor and floor landing is 3 inches or less
    B. post signs to that effect in the elevator car to warn passengers
    C. station a maintenance man near the ground floor stop to warn passengers
    D. take the car out of service during slow periods to make necessary adjustments

12. Although rock salt is commonly used on the walks when they are iced or heavily packed with snow, the *CHIEF* disadvantage of its use is that it

    A. creates a very slushy condition
    B. generally causes deterioration of concrete walks
    C. increases cleaning costs if used intensively
    D. is harmful to adjacent trees and shrubs

13. When instructing tenants how to clean enamel-painted woodwork, the tenant should be advised to wash the surfaces with

    A. ammonia water
    B. mild soap and water solution
    C. plain warm water
    D. strong soda solution

14. Of the following items included in the work schedule of porters, the one that should be assigned as a daily duty is

    A. cleaning incinerators
    B. cleaning stairhall windows and woodwork
    C. mopping all assigned stairhalls
    D. sweeping all stair landings

15. A building has a coal-fired steam boiler as the heating plant. While using the boiler, proper examination of the water gauge fails to reveal the presence of any water. Of the following, it would be best that

    A. a small amount of water be let into the boiler immediately, increasing the amount of water gradually until the proper level is reached
    B. the fire be put out immediately by covering with sand
    C. the fire be put out immediately by spraying with warm water
    D. the required amount of water be put into the boiler immediately

---

KEY (CORRECT ANSWERS)

1. D
2. C
3. C
4. D
5. D

6. C
7. B
8. B
9. C
10. D

11. D
12. D
13. B
14. D
15. B

EXAMINATION SECTION
TEST 1

DIRECTIONS: Each question or incomplete statement is followed by several suggested answers or completions. Select the one that BEST answers the question or completes the statement. *PRINT THE LETTER OF THE CORRECT ANSWER IN THE SPACE AT THE RIGHT.*

1. In a properly wired electrical circuit, the neutral wire is ALWAYS 1.____

    A. black or blue B. red or purple
    C. white or gray D. yellow or orange

2. A circuit breaker is a safety device in an electrical system and can BEST be described as performing the same function as a 2.____

    A. fuse B. limit switch
    C. relay D. thermostat

3. Which of the following is a difference between A.C. and D.C. electrical current? 3.____

    A. Ampere B. Cycle C. Volt D. Watt

4. Among the most common faults in providing electrical services is the furnishing of an inadequate number of outlets. 4.____
   Such a condition will LEAST likely result in

    A. higher bills for electricity
    B. hazardous use of extension wiring
    C. overheating of wires
    D. overloaded circuits

5. The force at which electricity is delivered is similar to pressure in a water supply system and is called 5.____

    A. amperage B. current C. wattage D. voltage

6. Which one of the following is NOT a general classification of windows? 6.____

    A. Awning B. Casement C. Sliding D. Expanding

7. All of the following are parts of a double-hung window EXCEPT the 7.____

    A. muntin B. saddle C. stile D. rail

8. Wooden obstructions placed between studs or floor joists to prevent fire from spreading in these natural flue spaces are called 8.____

    A. fire blocks B. fire walls
    C. fire stops D. flue dampers

9. Plaster is a mixture GENERALLY consisting of water, sand, and 9.____

    A. concrete B. gypsum
    C. aggregate D. calcium chloride

10. A parapet wall is that part of the masonry that extends above the roofline and is capped with noncombustible material.
    Of the following, one purpose a parapet wall does NOT serve is to

    A. strengthen the wall
    B. prevent people from falling off the roof
    C. prevent spread of fire
    D. provide a rest for fire department ladders

11. Large quantity purchasers of supplies and equipment often make their purchases on the basis of specifications. Which one of the following is NOT a good reason for using specifications?
    Specifications

    A. often offer a good description of what a product can do
    B. enable price comparisons since they set forth the price range to be paid for products
    C. set forth minimum standards that a product should meet
    D. enable the purchase of standardized products

12. The MAXIMUM permissible height of fences in residential districts in the city is _____ feet.

    A. 12   B. 10   C. 8   D. 6

13. A real estate manager under your supervision tells you that he is annoyed with some of his tenants who tend to lose their keys and then annoy the staff with requests for assistance.
    Which of the following suggestions should NOT be made to such tenants?

    A. Keep a duplicate set of keys at place of employment.
    B. Leave a duplicate set of keys with a friend or a relative.
    C. Put keys on a ring with name and address for prompt return if lost.
    D. Secure keys more firmly to the person by using a key chain or necklace.

14. An auxiliary lock is the simplest device to bolster the security offered by a primary door lock.
    Of the following, the STRONGEST type of auxiliary lock is usually the

    A. key-in-the-knob   B. thimble-groove
    C. trigger-bolt   D. vertical-bolt

15. In a multiple dwelling of nine or more dwelling units, where janitorial services are NOT performed on an approved 24-hour-a-day basis, the janitor MUST

    A. attend an approved course of instruction in the operation of low pressure boilers within three days of employment
    B. reside in or within a distance of one block or 200 feet, unless the owner resides in the multiple dwelling
    C. be licensed to operated low pressure boilers or have received a temporary permit therefor
    D. be a resident of the building or of an immediately adjoining building if the two buildings are under the same ownership

3 (#1)

16. The Multiple Dwelling Law permits the installation of a window security gate on a fire escape window.
In order to be acceptable in the city, the gate has to be stamped with a number indicating the approval of the Board of Standards and Appeals, should NOT require the use of a padlock, and MUST be

   A. openable from the inside without the use of a key
   B. constructed with a galvanized or other rust-proof finish
   C. connected to a sufficiently audible alarm device
   D. of the collapsible *accordion* type

17. A tenant tells you that she wishes to install a food waste disposer in her kitchen sink. You should inform her that

   A. such disposers are forbidden in the city because the sewage system cannot handle the additional waste load
   B. she is free to do so, provided the installation is done by a licensed plumber
   C. you will have the plumbing examined by a building inspector to make sure it is adequate in size
   D. within seven days after installation she must present to you a Certificate of Major Appliance Installation, duly notarized

18. When installing a new lighting fixture to replace an old one which is located in an outlet box, all of the following are safety precautions EXCEPT

   A. turning off the wall switch
   B. removing the fuse
   C. opening the circuit breaker
   D. replacing the bulb

19. During the heating season, landlords are required to maintain a minimum indoor temperature of 68° F. during the hours between 6 A.M. and 10 P.M. when the outdoor temperature falls below the allowable minimum temperature of

   A. 40° F   B. 45° F   C. 50° F   D. 55° F

20. When outside temperatures fall below certain levels, landlords are required to provide heat during the period from

   A. October 1 to April 30
   B. October 1 to May 31
   C. November 1 to April 30
   D. November 1 to May 31

21. In the city, many buildings have water tanks on the roof for all of the following reasons EXCEPT to

   A. furnish water for human consumption
   B. provide a water reserve for firefighting
   C. reduce stagnation in the water supply
   D. assure water pressure on the upper floors

22. A real estate manager was asked for his opinion on the purchase of a glass cutter. He recommended a steel wheel model rather than one with a carbide wheel.
    His advice was

    A. *poor;* mainly because the steel wheel is apt to cause the glass to splinter or break when it is used
    B. *good;* mainly because the steel wheel is less expensive
    C. *good;* mainly because the carbide wheel puts a sharper edge on the glass
    D. *poor;* mainly because the steel wheel is not all-purpose

23. Which of the following is GENERALLY an advantage of using alkyd paint rather than latex paint?
    It

    A. has better hiding power
    B. dries faster
    C. is easier to apply
    D. has less odor

24. In accordance with the Housing Maintenance Code, the central heating system of a multiple dwelling MUST be inspected by a qualified person at least

    A. in alternate years
    B. annually
    C. semi-annually
    D. quarterly

25. In accordance with the Housing Maintenance Code, hot water MUST generally be provided to tenants in a multiple dwelling between the hours of

    A. 5 A.M. and 10 P.M.
    B. 5 A.M. and 11 P.M.
    C. 6 A.M. and 9 P.M.
    D. 6 A.M. and Midnight

KEY (CORRECT ANSWERS)

1.	C	11.	B
2.	A	12.	D
3.	B	13.	C
4.	A	14.	D
5.	D	15.	B
6.	D	16.	A
7.	B	17.	A
8.	C	18.	D
9.	B	19.	D
10.	A	20.	B

21. C
22. B
23. A
24. B
25. D

TEST 2

DIRECTIONS: Each question or incomplete statement is followed by several suggested answers or completions. Select the one that BEST answers the question or completes the statement. *PRINT THE LETTER OF THE CORRECT ANSWER IN THE SPACE AT THE RIGHT.*

1. A tenant with whom you have dealt in the past comes to you with a question about general departmental policy. The tenant gives no reason for seeking this information. Of the following, the BEST way of dealing with him would usually be to

    A. answer his question and state the basis for the policy
    B. refrain from answering the question until he reveals his reason for asking it
    C. tell him that you cannot give him information for which he has no need
    D. withhold the information until you have discussed the matter with your superior

2. Notices or advertisements to sell real estate that contain the *seven basic facts* on properties usually bring better results.
   Of the following, which of these facts is considered LEAST important?

    A. Design
    B. Location
    C. Number of rooms
    D. Price and terms

3. According to the Sternlieb report (THE URBAN HOUSING DILEMMA: THE DYNAMICS OF NEW YORK CITY'S RENT CONTROLLED HOUSING), it was found that

    A. area disadvantages would not interfere with the availability of financing if rent control were removed
    B. the abolition of rent control would provide a solution to local housing problems, based on studies of other cities
    C. most of the low rent, rent-controlled buildings are owned by persons who own only one, or at most two, other buildings
    D. the income levels of rent-controlled buildings have made it impossible to maintain any of these buildings properly

4. A squatter is MOST NEARLY a tenant

    A. in fee simple   B. by the entirety
    C. in common   D. at sufferance

5. The new fire safety code for high-rise office buildings was the outcome of a study started after five persons died in high-rise fires.
   This code requires

    A. acquisition of additional fire damage and loss insurance wherever coverage is inadequate for full indemnification
    B. installation of devices to prevent automatic elevators from being drawn to floors where there is a fire
    C. installation of automatic sprinkler systems using foaming fire-extinguishing chemicals rather than water
    D. replacement of non-opening windows with removable panels offering ready access for firemen

6. With the increase in housing problems in the city, some tenant organizations have advocated and led rent strikes. Of the following, the BASIC reason for rent strikes is that the tenants involved

   A. want to force landlords to improve conditions in the buildings
   B. want court permission to withhold rent under the Real Property Actions and Proceedings Law
   C. have been encouraged to greater activism by the Legal Aid Society
   D. are already faced with dispossess action and have little to lose

7. A recent study by the city planning commission states that the MAIN reason that industries and business firms consider leaving the city is

   A. a lack of dependable employees
   B. their need for more space for expansion
   C. labor union disputes and high wages
   D. the increasing crime rate

8. The city's rent control law provides that certain *heads of households* over age 62 can

   A. be exempted from rent increase by filing for a rent exemption certificate
   B. receive exemption from decontrol provided they have custody of three or more minor children
   C. request and receive rent reductions if they agree to perform simple janitorial duties
   D. transfer possession of the premises to any person, and for any agreed-upon consideration

9. A person who, after the end of the term of a lease, retains possession as tenant of the property leased, is known as a

   A. freehold   B. holder in due course
   C. hold over   D. leasehold

10. When used in connection with fire or vandalism insurance, the term *deductible* refers to

    A. an amount that is noncompensable
    B. coverage sold through a pool
    C. optional modification of terms
    D. the full value of the loss

11. Tenants entering long-term leases for office space often rent more space than they need immediately in order to provide for future needs.
    With respect to such unused space, the USUAL practice of such tenants is to

    A. renegotiate the lease   B. seek a reduction
    C. sublet the space   D. delay expansion

12. The practice of temporarily relocating tenants into other housing within the same urban renewal area is USUALLY known as

    A. parceling   B. onsiting
    C. recycling   D. rotating

13. In the city, special zoning district regulations are used to control commercial real estate development in certain area locations.
In these districts, developers are permitted density bonuses if they

   A. provide plazas and other specified public amenities
   B. construct non-subsidized housing
   C. increase the total density through additional height
   D. consolidate non-contiguous plots

14. The Federal Housing Administration has, in recent years, become a major landlord.
The BASIC reason for this is that

   A. the Federal Housing Administration is operating low income leased housing programs
   B. major cities where housing is rapidly decaying have housing programs which are under exclusive Federal control
   C. the Federal Housing Administration has recently purchased depressed properties for possible future site use
   D. real estate speculators have sold many overpriced and defective homes whose mortgages were guaranteed and subsequently foreclosed by the Federal Housing Administration

15. Recently, it has been suggested that new housing, industrial, and recreational facilities be built on unused areas of the city's waterfront.
Of the following, the MAJOR obstacle to carrying out this proposal is

   A. a shortage of containerization facilities
   B. the difficulty in relocating displaced tenants
   C. the current overuse of the piers
   D. a lack of available financial support

16. A legal requirement that there be conspicuous notice provided to tenants in connection with the posting of notices would mean MOST NEARLY that the notice be

   A. posted by an employee in a conspicuous place
   B. posted in a place which is reasonably calculated to impart the information
   C. distributed so that each tenant receives a copy
   D. written in simplified English rather than the usual legalistic terminology

17. The city Board of Standards and Appeals determines appeals from certain administrative decisions of a number of city agencies.
The one of the following agencies whose decisions are NOT subject to review by the aforementioned Board is the

   A. Department of Buildings
   B. Department of Ports and Terminals
   C. Department of Tax Collection
   D. Fire Department

4 (#2)

18. Single-room occupants, usually poor, elderly and unemployable, have become an increasingly large problem in the city because of the steadily shrinking stock of single-room occupancy buildings.
The MAJOR reason for this decrease is that

   A. improved code enforcement by several city agencies has resulted in the shutting down of these unsafe buildings
   B. many single-room dwellings have been converted into small high-rental apartments or demolished under urban renewal
   C. much of this housing has been abandoned by owners who cannot, or will not, pay the taxes that have become due
   D. the demand for single rooms has been increased by an influx of single persons from other parts of the United States

19. Which of the following statements about the assessed valuation of real property in the city is MOST NEARLY correct?

   A. Each county determines rates for its jurisdiction.
   B. It has a relationship to the city's debt limit.
   C. It is generally considered to produce only minor revenue.
   D. Proposed changes are subject to a community referendum.

20. A Certificate of Eviction for a residential building erected prior to January 1, 1982 is USUALLY issued by the

   A. Department of Real Property Assessment
   B. Department of Relocation and Management Services
   C. Department of Rent and Housing Maintenance
   D. City Planning Commission

21. *In rem* buildings become the property of the city because of

   A. tax delinquency   B. condemnation
   C. public improvement   D. eminent domain

22. A non-profit membership corporation empowered to provide various services, including the improvement, development, repair, management, maintenance, and operation of real property acquired by the city in connection with urban renewal projects, is known as the

   A. City Urban Development Operations Corporation
   B. City Urban Renewal Management Corporation
   C. Urban Relocation Corporation
   D. Urban Resources Corporation

23. The designations *landmark* and *historic district,* when approved by the Landmarks Preservation Commission and ratified by the Board of Estimate, mean that

   A. exterior alterations to buildings cannot be made without prior approval of the Commission
   B. the Comptroller and Director of the Budget must agree jointly to the payment of city funds for improvements
   C. the premises must be open at reasonable times to guided tours conducted by the Commission
   D. neither exterior nor interior alterations may be made in any circumstances

24. The New York Plan is an agreement which involves the state, the city, and the building and construction industry.
Its MAIN purpose is to

   A. expedite the relocation of persons displaced by capital construction projects
   B. increase the dollar amount of non-residential building construction
   C. provide training and employment for minority group members
   D. reduce the amount of housing abandonment and subsequent receiverships

25. The State Labor Law provides that workers on any publicly assisted contract construction site MUST

   A. be paid the prevailing wages for their respective trades
   B. be members of a union approved by the Attorney General
   C. have completed a formal apprenticeship program
   D. receive wages for at least 215 days each year

Questions 26-35.

DIRECTIONS: Questions 26 through 35 are to be answered on the basis of the following tables, which contain data concerning the Green Valley Region, a fictional area.

HOUSING PATTERNS, GREEN VALLEY REGION 1990-2000

TABLE I

TYPE OF HOUSING	SUBURBS		TOWNS		REGION TOTAL*	
	1990	2000	1990	2000	1990	2000
Multi-Unit Dwellings	2,600	5,200	9,300	10,900	13,700	18,800
Single-Unit Dwellings	15,100	17,700	11,000	11,400	43,700	46,900
Mobile Dwellings	300	?	900	1,800	14,700	31,400
TOTAL	18,000	23,600	21,200	24,100	72,100	97,100

*NOTE: Region totals include other categories in addition to suburbs and towns.

TABLE II
SUBSTANDARD HOUSING, GREEN VALLEY REGION
(INCLUDED IN FIGURES IN TABLE I, ABOVE)

	1990-800 UNITS	2000-1,200 UNITS
Multi-Unit	64%	54%
Single-Unit	33%	28%
Mobile	3%	18%

26. If the single-unit dwellings in towns in 1990 each contained an average of 5.1 rooms, the total number of rooms in this category was MOST NEARLY

   A. 56,000   B. 61,000   C. 561,000   D. 651,000

27. The number of mobile dwellings in the suburbs in 2000 was

   A. 500   B. 600   C. 700   D. 800

28. From 1990 to 2000, the total number of all Green Valley Region housing units increased by MOST NEARLY

    A. 31%   B. 34%   C. 37%   D. 40%

29. For 2000, what was the TOTAL number of substandard multi-unit dwellings?

    A. 548   B. 573   C. 623   D. 648

30. In the towns, from 1990 to 2000, the type of housing having the LARGEST proportionate increase was

    A. mobile
    B. multi-unit
    C. single-unit
    D. substandard

31. In 2000, the TOTAL number of dwellings which were not substandard was

    A. 95,300   B. 95,900   C. 96,200   D. 96,500

32. Assume that, in 1990, 3.5 persons was the average occupancy in the towns in each kind of dwelling.
    Thus, the population of the towns in the Green Valley Region in 1990 was

    A. 73,600   B. 73,800   C. 74,000   D. 74,200

33. Which of the following statements concerning mobile dwellings is CORRECT?

    A. In 2000, mobile dwellings were the largest category of substandard dwellings.
    B. In 1990, the number of mobile dwellings in suburbs was greater by *30%* than the number in towns.
    C. In the Green Valley Region during the period 1990-2000, the number of mobile dwellings increased by 50%.
    D. In 1990, the total number of mobile dwellings in the Green Valley Region was less than 25% of the total number of all dwellings.

34. Assume that, of the single-unit dwellings not in suburbs and towns in 1990, 20% were in villages.
    Therefore, the number of single-unit dwellings in villages in 1990 was

    A. 2,480   B. 3,070   C. 3,520   D. 4,110

35. Assume that in the Green Valley Region, the following changes are expected in 2010 as compared to 2000: the number of suburban dwellings will increase by 30%; the number of town dwellings will decrease by 15%. Therefore, the ratio of suburban dwellings to town dwellings expected for 2010 is MOST NEARLY

    A. 3 to 2   B. 4 to 3   C. 5 to 4   D. 6 to 5

Questions 36-38.

DIRECTIONS: Questions 36 through 38 are to be answered on the basis of the following paragraph.

In recent years, new and important emphasis has been placed upon the maximum use of conservation and rehabilitation techniques in carrying out programs of urban renewal and revitalization. In urban renewal projects where existing structures are hopelessly deteriorated or land uses are incompatible with the community's overall plans, the entire area may be *acquired, cleared, and sold for redevelopment. However, where existing structures are basically sound but have deteriorated to the point where they are a <u>blighting</u> influence on the neighborhood, they may be salvaged through a program of rehabilitation and reconditioning.*

36. According to the above paragraph, the one of the following which is MOST likely to cause area-wide razing of the buildings in urban renewal programs is

    A. a program of rehabilitation and reconditioning
    B. concerted insistence by landlords and tenants that certain buildings be bulldozed
    C. an inability of community groups to agree on priorities for staged clearance
    D. land use contrary to the community's general plan

37. According to the above paragraph, rehabilitation of structures may take place if

    A. new conservation and rehabilitation techniques are used
    B. salvaging all the buildings in the entire area is hopeless
    C. the community wishes to preserve historic structures
    D. the existing buildings are structurally sound

38. As used in the above paragraph, the word *blighting* means MOST NEARLY

    A. ruining
    B. infrequent
    C. recurrent
    D. traditional

Questions 39-42.

DIRECTIONS: Questions 39 through 42 are to be answered SOLELY on the basis of the following paragraph.

The concentration of publicly assisted housing in central cities -- because the suburbs do not want them and effectively bar them -- is usually <u>rationalized</u> by a solicitous regard for keeping intact the city neighborhoods cherished by low-income groups. If one accepted this as valid, the devotion of minorities to blighted city neighborhoods in preference to suburban employment and housing would be an historic first. Certainly no such devotion was visible among the millions who have deserted their city neighborhoods in the last 25 years even if it meant an arduous daily trip from the suburbs to their jobs in the cities.

39. The writer implies that MOST poor people

    A. prefer isolation
    B. fear change
    C. are angry
    D. seek betterment

40. The general tone of the paragraph is BEST characterized as

    A. uncertain
    B. skeptical
    C. evasive
    D. indifferent

41. As used in the above paragraph, the word *rationalize* means MOST NEARLY

    A. dispute   B. justify   C. deny   D. locate

42. According to the above paragraph, publicly assisted housing is concentrated in the central cities PRIMARILY because   42.____

    A. city dwellers are unable to find satisfactory housing
    B. deterioration of older housing has increased in recent years
    C. suburbanites have opposed the movement of the poor to the suburbs
    D. employment opportunities have decreased in the suburbs

Questions 43-46.

DIRECTIONS: Questions 43 through 46 are to be answered SOLELY on the basis of the following paragraph.

A city may expand by growing vertically through the replacement of lower buildings with higher ones; or by filling in open spaces between settled areas; or by extending the existing settled area. When the settled area is expanded, growth may take several forms, the most important forms being concentric circle or ring growth around the central nucleus; axial growth, with prongs or finger-like extensions moving out along main transportation routes; and suburban growth, with the establishment of islands of settlements before the expansion of the main city area. These types of expansion are characteristic of most large cities. Baltimore was for a long time a good example of ring growth, whereas New York, Chicago, and Detroit illustrate axial and suburban growth.

43. The title that BEST expresses the theme of this paragraph is   43.____

    A. FORMS OF CITY EXPANSION
    B. MAJOR METROPOLITAN PROBLEMS
    C. METHODS OF URBAN PLANNING
    D. SUBURBAN GROWTH IN AMERICA

44. The one of the following which is example of vertical growth is the   44.____

    A. settlement of year-round residents along the upper Hudson River
    B. restoration of former rooming houses to their original brownstone condition
    C. subdivision of large estates into small lot semidetached houses
    D. erection of the World Trade Center in New York City

45. A city that grew as a concentric circle is   45.____

    A. Baltimore   B. New York   C. Chicago   D. Detroit

46. When the author speaks of axial growth, he refers to a situation where   46.____

    A. expansion is primarily into rural areas until suburbs are thereby created
    B. small towns and villages are consolidated by gradually growing until one large city is created
    C. the direction in which a city expands is determined by the location of major highways
    D. the number of new buildings is greater than the number of old buildings demolished

Questions 47-50.

DIRECTIONS: Questions 47 through 50 are to be answered SOLELY on the basis of the following paragraph.

Although the suburbs have provided housing and employment for millions of additional families since 1970, many suburban communities have maintained controls over the kinds of families who can live in them. Suburban attitudes have been formed by reaction against a perception of crowded, harassed city life and threatening alien city people. As population, taxable income, and jobs have left the cities for the suburbs, the "urban crisis" of substandard housing, declining levels of education and public services, and decreasing employment opportunities has been created. The crisis, however, is not urban at all, but national, and in part a result of the suburban policy that discourages outward movement by the urban poor.

47. According to the above paragraph, the quality of urban life

    A. is determined by public opinion in the cities
    B. has worsened in recent years
    C. is similar to rural life
    D. can be changed by political means

48. According to the above paragraph, suburban communities have

    A. tried to show that the urban crisis is really a national crisis
    B. avoided taking a position on the urban crisis
    C. been involved in causing the urban crisis
    D. been the innocent victims of the urban crisis

49. According to the above paragraph, the poor have

    A. become increasingly sophisticated in their attempts to move to the suburbs
    B. generally been excluded from the suburbs
    C. lost incentive for betterment of their living conditions
    D. sought improvement of the central cities

50. As used in the above paragraph, the word *perception* means MOST NEARLY

    A. development   B. impression
    C. opposition   D. uncertainty

KEY (CORRECT ANSWERS)

1. A	11. C	21. A	31. B	41. B
2. A	12. B	22. B	32. D	42. D
3. C	13. A	23. A	33. D	43. A
4. D	14. D	24. C	34. C	44. D
5. B	15. D	25. A	35. A	45. A
6. A	16. B	26. A	36. D	46. C
7. B	17. C	27. C	37. D	47. B
8. A	18. B	28. B	38. A	48. C
9. C	19. B	29. D	39. D	49. B
10. A	20. C	30. A	40. B	50. B

TEST 3

DIRECTIONS: Each question or incomplete statement is followed by several suggested answers or completions. Select the one that BEST answers the question or completes the statement. *PRINT THE LETTER OF THE CORRECT ANSWER IN THE SPACE AT THE RIGHT.*

1. In awarding contracts for maintenance repair work, the MOST important rule to follow is to 1.____

    A. judge on competitive bidding, based on written specifications
    B. prequalify the bidders, based only on length of time in business
    C. require bidding and payment bonds from all bidders
    D. require performance bonds from all bidders

2. Which one of the following methods is MOST effective for monitoring the performance of large maintenance contracts? 2.____

    A. Establishing a percentage retainer as work is completed by submittal of invoices.
    B. Having contractor attest to amount of work performed.
    C. Requiring performance bonds and placing responsibility on bonding company.
    D. Spot-checking of work, performed by inspectors who are rotated.

3. The one of the following that MOST frequently occurs when a plug fuse blows is that the 3.____

    A. isinglass window melts
    B. mica window cracks
    C. window of the fuse blackens
    D. window of the fuse turns blue

4. If 20-ampere fuses in a 20-ampere circuit in an electric lighting panel repeatedly blow out, the BEST action to take is t 4.____

    A. install a ground fault interrupter
    B. install a fuse having a higher ampere rating
    C. trouble-shoot the circuit before replacing the fuse
    D. replace the fuse with a solid copper bar

5. One of the BASIC parts of a stairway is the 5.____

    A. apron   B. soffit   C. stool   D. threshold

6. A plumbing trap is a device used in a waste system to 6.____

    A. facilitate the waste discharge from plumbing fixtures
    B. limit the discharge of waste
    C. prevent backflow to a water main
    D. prevent the passage of sewer gas into the building

7. Gas-fueled or electric space or water heaters, where permitted by law in a multiple dwelling, are required to

   A. be installed by the owner according to the wishes of the tenant as to capacity, number, and location
   B. furnish the same standard of heat or hot water supply as is required to be furnished from a central heat or hot water system
   C. be operated so that the owner of the building is solely responsible for the full cost of the gas or electricity used by such heaters
   D. be repaired and maintained by the tenant with no charge or liability to the landlord or his agent

8. At what point is the water supply system to a building USUALLY shut off by a municipality?
   At the

   A. house wall
   B. corporation cock
   C. house basement
   D. meter

9. A float and thermostat trap is a part of which of the following piping systems? _____ system.

   A. Cold water
   B. Hot water
   C. Steam heating
   D. Waste line

10. Air chambers are built into plumbing systems to

    A. decrease water flow
    B. filter out water-borne sand
    C. inhibit rust formation
    D. reduce water hammer

11. On which type of heating system is a plenum chamber used?

    A. Hot air
    B. Hot water
    C. One-pipe steam
    D. Two-pipe steam

12. Heating boilers may be classified according to several kinds of characteristics. All of the following are types of boilers EXCEPT

    A. radiator
    B. Scotch marine
    C. sectional
    D. water-tube

13. In a large multiple dwelling, under properly controlled maintenance conditions, it would be BEST to use fuel oil which is classified as grade number

    A. 2   B. 3   C. 4   D. 6

14. For proper service, vapor barriers used in roofs and exterior walls of buildings should NOT be made of

    A. asphalted paper
    B. canvas
    C. metal foil
    D. plastic

15. According to the housing maintenance code, in a room located on the top story of a converted dwelling, a skylight

    A. of the proper dimensions may be substituted for a required window
    B. is not permissible except in fire-proof buildings
    C. is allowable as a means of emergency exit in lieu of a fire escape provided an adequate ladder is installed
    D. is forbidden in all dwelling units

16. Provisions for non-conforming uses put into zoning ordinances ordinarily prohibit all of the following EXCEPT the

    A. enlargement or expansion of a non-conforming use
    B. changing the non-conforming use to any other non-conforming use
    C. continuance of an established non-conforming use
    D. complete reconstruction of the non-conforming use

17. Permission to do some act contrary to a zoning ordinance is known as a(n)

    A. encroachment   B. indenture
    C. ordinance   D. variance

18. The custodian of a group of buildings had, in his office, a large pegboard which holds duplicate keys for all his tenants. He tagged the keys with coded numbers instead of the actual apartment designations.
    The use of coded keys is USUALLY considered to be

    A. *good;* it allows keys to be more quickly located
    B. *good;* it reduces the danger of misuse of keys
    C. *bad;* it requires an additional cost in handling keys
    D. *bad;* tenants will be unable to recognize their keys

19. Until recently, it was unlawful to have bars or gates on a fire escape window.
    Now, the law permits the installation of a security gate or device, provided that it has stamped on it a Board of Standards and Appeals number and it

    A. uses only an approved padlock which can be opened only from the inside with the use of a key
    B. does not require any type of padlock and can be opened from the inside with the use of a key
    C. uses only an approved padlock which can be opened from either side with the use of a key
    D. does not require any type of padlock and can be opened from the inside without the use of a key

20. Mortise locks provide more security than key-in-the-knob locks because MOST of the locking mechanism of a mortise lock is

    A. accessible from outside the door
    B. enclosed in the beveled convenience latch
    C. located in a metal enclosure in the door, rather than in the knob
    D. removable for adjustment and repair

21. A tenant installed on his door a special lock of the double cylinder type. This type of lock can be locked with a key from the inside.
    The major DISADVANTAGE of such a lock is that

    A. a skillful burglar would be able to open it more quickly
    B. in a fire or other emergency a key may not be available to open the door from the inside
    C. it is a violation of both state and city laws and regulations
    D. when repairs are necessary, access to the inside cylinder is difficult

22. It is generally agreed that the BEST protection for most kinds of buildings against prowlers and thieves is provided by

    A. a bell, buzzer, and voice intercommunication system
    B. a well-trained security and maintenance staff
    C. closed-circuit television and convex mirrors
    D. locks of some kind on all doors

23. During the heating season, landlords are required to maintain a minimum indoor temperature of 55° F. during the hours between 10 P.M. to 6 A.M., when the outdoor temperature falls below the allowable minimum point of

    A. 30° F.   B. 35° F.   C. 40° F.   D. 45° F.

24. According to the BEST practice, a minor change in a lease between landlord and tenant

    A. should be agreed to orally provided that a witness is present
    B. must have a special form which should be securely affixed to the original lease
    C. should be put in writing as part of the lease and signed by both parties
    D. should not be made unless the circumstances are exceptional since such changes require court approval

25. Housing units that are completely finished at a factory, including installation of wiring, plumbing, and carpeting, and are usually ready for occupancy except for major utilities, are known as _____ units.

    A. cluster   B. modular
    C. intrinsic   D. quadplex

26. The owner of a multiple dwelling must paint every fire escape with two coats of paint in contrasting colors. The requirement that two colors be used

    A. is based on the fact that two colors will provide greater protection to the metal
    B. facilitates scraping and removal of the paint after the mandatory period of five years
    C. is for the purpose of combining the first color with the second color to provide a neutral tone
    D. allows for inspection and verification that two coats of paint were actually used

27. The term *key money* refers to

   A. so-called *seed money* used to reduce the amount of money borrowed to finance residential construction
   B. the difference between the controlled rent for a given apartment and the rent such an apartment would bring if uncontrolled
   C. the *fee,* or bribe, demanded of a prospective tenant by someone in a position to provide an apartment
   D. cooperative maintenance charges which are at a level that middle-income families can afford

28. The principle of independence of covenants rather than interdependence of covenants applies to a landlord-tenant lease, according to real property law.
   The effect of this independence of covenants is that NEARLY ALWAYS

   A. the tenant is required to consult an attorney prior to entering into a long-term lease
   B. the tenant must continue to pay rent even if customary services are interrupted
   C. landlords are placed under great pressure to modify lease terms even after they have been agreed to
   D. landlords will ask tenants to sign a statement reading *I solemnly affirm that I have read and fully understand the terms of this lease*

29. A condition which is inserted in a deed, lease, mortgage, or contract, and on the performance or non-performance of which the validity of the instrument USUALLY depends, is known as a

   A. pendency
   B. prima facie
   C. pro tempore
   D. proviso

30. A landlord, without intent to oust a tenant, commits an act which deprives the tenant of the beneficial enjoyment of the premises, and the tenant voluntarily gives up possession. Such a situation is known as

   A. destructive conversion
   B. homestead exemption
   C. constructive eviction
   D. due reversion

31. The term *class action,* used in a lawsuit brought against a landlord, means MOST NEARLY that the lawsuit is an action brought on behalf of

   A. a low-income economic group
   B. an ethnic minority group
   C. elderly rent-controlled tenants
   D. persons similarly situated

32. In a public or private housing development which has admission rules concerning income level, the amount above the basic rent that must be paid by a tenant whose income rises above such level is USUALLY known as a

   A. balance
   B. net overage
   C. surcharge
   D. voluntary assessment

33. The one of the following which is USUALLY included in a standard residential lease is

   A. a description of premises
   B. a guarantee of habitability
   C. the right to deduct repair costs
   D. a 90-day right to cancel

34. Assume that a landlord, wishing to stop a tenant from committing a nuisance on the landlord's property, seeks a court order.
    The court order would GENERALLY be referred to as a(n)

   A. injunction   B. writ of mandamus
   C. real estate estoppel   D. tenant referral

35. State legislation prohibits real estate brokers from using racial considerations to frighten homeowners into selling.
    Nevertheless, city officials have urged the passage of even stricter legislation against such *blockbusting* MAINLY because, as matters now stand,

   A. brokers can still break up neighborhoods by warning of declining property values, without specifically referring to any minority group
   B. real estate associations are united in their support of blockbusting tactics
   C. homeowners are fearful of reporting instances of blockbusting due to the severe penalties of the law for conspiring with blockbusters
   D. fraudulent unsworn testimony is freely accepted at public hearings without any penalties for false statements, since testimony need not be sworn to

36. Use and occupancy insurance is insurance that protects against loss of

   A. gross receipts following an unprovoked termination of lease
   B. net income resulting from condemnation
   C. rent resulting from destruction of a building
   D. things substantial and immovable

37. The MAIN advantage for the purchaser of real estate title insurance is that such insurance generally

   A. guarantees that the terms of mortgage agreements will be complied with
   B. pays for damages resulting from defects in title
   C. guarantees that no restrictions will be placed upon property in the future
   D. guarantees that the insurer will take title to the property in the event of hidden defects

38. An IMPORTANT advantage of building attached homes with common party walls is that

   A. construction of this type encourages long-term tenancy
   B. higher land costs can be supported
   C. occupants are less likely to make demands on owners or real estate managers
   D. such homes are particularly resistive to the spread of fire

39. Guidelines designed to end sex discrimination in employment were recently issued by the city government for the information of contractors doing business with the city. These guidelines call on contractors to do all of the following EXCEPT to

   A. abolish all job duties that require extraordinary physical strength
   B. base qualifications for employment solely on ability or performance
   C. eliminate from employment applications questions about marital or parental status
   D. remove sex-based restrictive titles from job descriptions

39.____

40. The U.S. Department of Housing and Urban Development has set up a direct-dial, toll-free Washington telephone number of public use in reporting housing discrimination. Which of the following statements states the reason given by the Department of Housing and Urban Development?

   A. Although housing discrimination has generally been eliminated, and most persons know how to secure their rights, vigilance is always necessary.
   B. Housing discrimination continues, primarily because many persons do not know about the law, nor do they know how and where to report if they meet discrimination.
   C. Irrespective of the existence or non-existence of housing discrimination, a public relations program should be based upon image.
   D. Whether housing discrimination is or is not illusory, a certain segment of society will always require solicitous and understanding treatment.

40.____

41. The number of rent-stabilized apartments in the city is _____ the number of rent-controlled apartments.

   A. based on a fixed ratio to
   B. about the same as
   C. greater than
   D. less than

41.____

42. The court which has landlord and tenant parts is the

   A. Civil Court   B. Court of Appeals
   C. Criminal Court   D. Family Court

42.____

43. A city Mitchell-Lama rental development received tax and mortgage benefits from the city.
However, as a requirement for obtaining such benefits, the development had to

   A. join the city-wide tenants' council
   B. grant priority in admission to city residents
   C. make payments into the city's general fund
   D. allow strict city supervision and regulation, especially of rents

43.____

44. An organization that is privately owned but is subject to control by the Federal government, and which stimulates mortgage lending, is the

   A. Federal Housing Administration
   B. Federal National Mortgage Association
   C. Real Property Lending Association
   D. National Housing Mortgage Association

44.____

45. The present building code is different from the former code PRIMARILY in that, under the present code, building materials

    A. are listed in order according to degree of acceptability
    B. must meet standards developed by the Department of Purchase
    C. must meet specified performance test standards
    D. that will be developed in the future are to eliminate metal as far as possible

46. Appeals from real property tax assessments in the city are heard FIRST by the

    A. Board of Estimate
    B. Board of Standards and Appeals
    C. Budget Commission
    D. Tax Commission

47. The Rent Stabilization Law requires that at least 35% of the tenants of an eligible building agree to purchase their apartments before the building can be converted to a cooperative. Some critics, however, advocate raising the minimum number who must agree to 51%. They claim that the tenants would benefit.
    Of the following, the MAJOR benefit to the tenants is MOST likely to be that

    A. increasing the number of tenants consenting would provide more money to reduce monthly maintenance costs
    B. the owner's terms may be lower if he must bargain with more tenants
    C. the owner could more promptly complete the transaction since more cash would be available to him
    D. the sale would be more easily completed since the rest of the tenants would be more likely to join the majority consenting

48. In an R-10 zone, the city's highest residential density, 10 square feet of floor area is allowed for each square foot of land.
    In addition, a bonus of 20% is obtainable for

    A. maximum use of architectural metals
    B. keeping return on equity constant
    C. providing open plazas at street level
    D. buildings which are used by wholesalers

49. In the city, buildings with out-of-order water meters are not billed for water until meters are repaired.
    The result of such non-billing is that

    A. bills for estate taxes are held up
    B. no accurate knowledge of water use exists, with the result that a possible water shortage might not be promptly detected
    C. it can be advantageous for violators not to comply with official requests to repair meters since, in effect, they obtain interest-free loans from the city
    D. the water meter readers lack adequate and timely information about ownership and general classification of buildings

50. The recent public outcry against the use of asbestos in fire-proofing steel beams is based upon the fact that	50.____

   A. airborne asbestos particles cause slippery dust granules to settle over many parts of the city
   B. increasing construction costs could be significantly reduced by substituting other materials
   C. inhalation of asbestos is associated with an increased incidence of cancer
   D. water damage in skyscraper fires can be reduced by more effective means

KEY (CORRECT ANSWERS)

1. A	11. A	21. B	31. D	41. D
2. D	12. A	22. B	32. C	42. A
3. C	13. D	23. C	33. A	43. D
4. C	14. B	24. C	34. A	44. B
5. B	15. A	25. B	35. A	45. C
6. D	16. C	26. D	36. C	46. D
7. B	17. D	27. C	37. B	47. B
8. B	18. B	28. B	38. B	48. C
9. C	19. D	29. D	39. A	49. C
10. D	20. C	30. C	40. B	50. C

EXAMINATION SECTION
TEST 1

DIRECTIONS: Each question or incomplete statement is followed by several suggested answers or completions. Select the one that BEST answers the question or completes the statement. *PRINT THE LETTER OF THE CORRECT ANSWER IN THE SPACE AT THE RIGHT.*

1. During an interview with a tenant at your office, he confides to you that he would rather find his own apartment for his family than move into public housing. He asks for your advice in this matter.
   The BEST thing you can do is

   A. advise that he look only to public housing since these are the best apartments
   B. tell him that you cannot advise him in such personal matters and then refer him to Social Services
   C. discuss with him the different ways he might find an apartment, including one in public housing
   D. suggest that he talk over his decision more carefully with his family

2. While inspecting conditions around a site, you notice that some of the garbage cans are not covered.
   Which of the following BEST explains why this condition should be corrected? To

   A. prevent the garbage cans from getting lost
   B. prevent garbage from cans spreading onto the street
   C. allow sanitation men to handle the cans without spillage
   D. keep dogs and cats from knocking garbage cans over

3. While interviewing tenants, an assistant may find that a tenant will be silent for a short time before answering questions.
   In order to get the required information from the tenant when this happens, the assistant should GENERALLY

   A. repeat the same question to make the tenant stop hesitating
   B. ask the tenant to write out his answer
   C. ask the tenant to answer quickly because other tenants are waiting to see you
   D. wait patiently and not pressure the tenant into quick, undeveloped answers

4. A tenant that you have been trying to encourage to apply for public housing comes to your desk at the site office. He is talking in a very angry and excited way about the lack of heat in his apartment. He says he will not pay his rent until there is heat.
   The BEST thing for you to do at this time is to

   A. tell him that he should have applied for public housing as you suggested
   B. immediately let your supervisor know that he is refusing to pay his rent
   C. let him talk until he finishes and then discuss his problem with him
   D. tell him that you will not talk to him until he stops yelling

5. You have been informed that no determination has yet been made on the eligibility of a certain tenant for public housing. The decision will depend upon further checking. When you see the tenant, he seems to be quite worried, and he asks you whether his application has been accepted.
   What would be BEST for you to do under these circumstances? Tell him

   A. you can't talk to him because there is no definite information and you are very busy
   B. to put his question in writing and send it to your manager so that it will be on record
   C. you don't know yet but that he should not worry since you are quite sure he will be accepted
   D. his application is being checked, and you will let him know the final result

6. An assistant is interviewing a high priority applicant who, contrary to usual experience, is extremely well-prepared and supplied with all the information the assistant is seeking. Which of the following possible actions by the assistant is MOST suitable under these circumstances?

   A. Directly showing a willingness to review the information carefully and promptly
   B. Exercising extreme caution about the credibility of the facts presented
   C. Showing his awareness that the applicant is trying to trick him with false information
   D. Accepting all of the candidate's information because of his obviously high level of intelligence

7. One of the tenants to be relocated is an extremely alert but elderly man who resists your every attempt to discuss with him the necessity for moving. He has lived in this building for almost thirty years, and he states flatly that he will NOT move.
   Of the following, the MOST acceptable action for you to take is to

   A. tell him he is being unreasonable and selfish
   B. forcibly have him removed from the premises
   C. refer his case to a social worker
   D. advise him to take his case to the Legal Aid Society

8. Suppose you telephone to set up an important appointment with a tenant for a specific day on your calendar. He refuses to meet with you on that day because he claims the day is his religious holiday.
   What is the BEST way of handling this situation?

   A. Tell him it is against his interest not to meet with you on that day
   B. Give up any idea now of meeting with him and go on to arranging your next appointment
   C. Ask when he will be able to meet with you and indicate to him what the subject is
   D. Indicate to him that you know the holiday cannot be important since city employees do not officially have that day off

9. In a building slated for demolition but still inhabited by tenants, an assistant sees some children of tenants pulling on a pipe in the hall. He tells them to stop but they say that the building is being torn down anyway. What should the assistant do FIRST?

   A. Explain to the children that although this is true, they are causing danger to tenants still in the building.

B. Go immediately to the parents and tell them to punish their children for their misbehavior.
C. Say nothing else to the children but go to the site office and report the problem to his supervisor.
D. Go outside and call a policeman but tell the policeman to treat the children gently.

10. When interviewing a tenant who is to be relocated, the FIRST of the following actions for you to take is to

    A. inform the tenant that your office will help only if he cooperates
    B. advise the tenant that you must see proof for all statements he makes
    C. assure the tenant that every effort will be made to find suitable housing
    D. tell the tenant he will have no trouble finding new housing facilities

11. During interviews, people give information about themselves in several ways.
    Of the following, which would usually give the LEAST amount of information about the person being questioned? His

    A. spoken words
    B. tone of voice
    C. facial expression
    D. body position

12. Suppose that while you are interviewing a tenant about the condition of his apartment, he becomes angered by your questioning and begins to use abusive language. Which of the following is the BEST way for you to react to him?

    A. Use the same kind of language as he does to show him that you are neither impressed nor upset by his speech.
    B. Interrupt him and tell him that you are not required to listen to such language.
    C. Lower your voice and speak more slowly in an attempt to set an example that will calm him.
    D. Let him continue to use abusive language but insist that he answer your questions at once.

13. Of the following characteristics, the one which would be MOST helpful for an assistant when helping an angry applicant understand why he has been turned down for public housing would be the ability to

    A. state the rules exactly as they are written
    B. show examples of other cases where the same thing happened
    C. remain patient and understanding of the person's position
    D. remain uninvolved and cold to individual personal problems

Questions 14-19.

DIRECTIONS: Answer Questions 14 through 19 on the basis of the information given in the paragraphs below.

Three year's ago, a city introduced a program of reduced transit rates for the elderly. It was hoped that this program would increase the travel of the elderly and help them maintain a greater measure of independence. About 600,000 of the 800,000 eligible residents are currently enrolled in the program. To be eligible, a person must be 65 years of age or older and not employed full-time. Riding for reduced fare is permitted between 10:00 M. and 4:00 P.M. and between 7:00 P.M. and midnight on weekdays and 24 hours a day on Saturdays, Sundays, and holidays.

In a city university study based on a sampling of 728 enrollees interviewed, it was learned that 51 percent are able to travel more, and 30.8 percent had been able to save enough money to make a noticeable difference in their budgets as a result of the reduced-fare program.

It has been recommended that reduced-fare programs be extended to encourage the use of transit Lines in off-hours by other groups such as the poor, the very young, housewives, and the physically handicapped. To implement this recommendation, it would be necessary for the Federal government to increase transit subsidies.

14. Which one of the following would be the BEST title for the passage above?

    A. A Program of Reduced Transit Rates for the Elderly
    B. Recommendations for Extending Programs for the Elderly
    C. City University Study on the Relationship of Age and Travel
    D. Eligibility Requirements for the Reduced Rate Program

15. *Approximately* what percentage of the eligible residents is currently enrolled in the reduced-fare program?

    A. 25%   B. 50%   C. 65%   D. 75%

16. Which one of the following persons is NOT eligible for the reduced-fare program? A

    A. Woman, age 67, employed part-time as a stenographer
    B. Handicapped man, age 62
    C. Blind man, age 66, employed part-time as a transcribing typist
    D. Housewife, age 70

17. At which one of the following times would the reduced-fare NOT be permitted for an eligible elderly person?

    A. Sunday, 6:00 P.M.   B. Christmas Day, 2:00 M.
    C. Tuesday, 9:00 M.   D. Thursday, 8:00 P.M.

18. Of the 728 enrollees interviewed in a city university study of the reduced-fare program, it was found that

    A. the majority traveled more and saved money at the same time
    B. more than half traveled less and therefore saved money
    C. about half traveled more and. about one-third saved money
    D. the majority saved money but traveled the same rate as before

19. According to the passage above, what would be necessary to extend the reduced-fare program to other groups of people?

   A. Increasing the eligible age to 68
   B. Reducing the hours when half-fare is permitted
   C. Increasing the fare for other riders
   D. Increasing the transit subsidies by the Federal government

20. Reports are made MOST often in order to

   A. suggest new ideas
   B. give information
   C. issue orders to workers
   D. show that work is being done

21. An assistant is reporting a loose floor board in a certain apartment building on the site. The MOST important thing he should report in order to get immediate repairs is

   A. how the floor board became loose
   B. when the floor board became loose
   C. the type of material and the number of men needed to make the repair
   D. in which apartment the loose floor board is located

22. Suppose you receive a phone call from a tenant about a problem that requires you to look up the information and call her back. Although the tenant had given you her name earlier and you can say the name, you are not sure that you can spell it correctly. Which of the following would be MOST likely to insure that you spell the name correctly?

   A. Say the name slowly and ask her if you are saying it correctly.
   B. Spell her name as you have been saying it.
   C. Ask her to spell the name so that you can write it.
   D. Look through your files for a similar name and copy the spelling.

23. When tenants relocate, a report is made. This report is in the form of a standard form instead of a fully written report.
    The MOST important advantage of using a standard form for certain information is that

   A. one can be sure that the report will be sent in as soon as possible
   B. anyone can write out the report without directions from a supervisor
   C. needed information is less likely to be left out of the report
   D. information that is written up this way is less likely to be false

24. Suppose you are filling out a section of a form to describe an incident which will be read by a social worker but you run out of space before finishing. It would be BEST for you to

   A. leave out whatever information you consider unimportant
   B. write what you can on the form and attach another sheet with the rest of the information
   C. cross out what you wrote on the form and write on a separate sheet of paper which you attach to the form
   D. write what you can on the form and tell your supervisor or the social worker the rest of it

25. It is part of an assistant's job to help a manager enter various items of information on a monthly report. This information may be, for example, the number of tenants relocated to different types of housing and the number of tenants left on the site.
The assistant must be careful NOT to make mistakes on his entries about tenants because

A. mistakes will show his supervisor that his work is poor
B. records must not be too difficult to read
C. these mistakes are hard to notice and correct
D. correct records are needed for the department to operate smoothly

26. For tenants who are not eligible for public housing and who are unable to find a new apartment, the relocation agency

A. refers the case to the Human Rights Commission
B. seeks to obtain private housing for the family
C. advises the family to move in with relatives and friends
D. arranges sleeping quarters at the site office

27. The MAXIMUM amount of money a relocated family can receive for moving expenses is

A. under $500
B. $500 - 750
C. $751 - 1000
D. $1001 - 1500

28. Of the following conditions that are often present in slum buildings, the one which is MOST likely to cause lead poisoning in children is

A. exposed rusty nails in floors
B. uncovered garbage cans containing old pencils
C. paint flaking off walls and window sills
D. the escape of fumes from faulty oil burners

29. An assistant would be correct to advise a tenant that it is ILLEGAL to throw which of the following into an incinerator?

A. Compactly wrapped bundles
B. Empty plastic bags
C. Loose vacuum or carpet sweepings
D. Soapy rags

30. A housing project is being built on Site X.
Of the following, the people who are given priority for apartments in the project if they meet eligibility requirements are

A. former tenants of Site X
B. welfare recipients
C. minority groups with the lowest income
D. families with the most children

31. A family which occupied a 4 1/2 room apartment at an urban renewal site moved to an off-site 5-room apartment. They were eligible for a 6-room apartment, but it was unavailable.
The family is now entitled to reimbursement for moving expenses based on

A. a 4-room apartment
B. a 5-room apartment
C. a 6-room apartment
D. actual cost of the move in an unlimited amount

32. During inspection of a tenant's apartment, you observe that the grids and burners of the stove are greasy and heavily caked with spilled food. Because of this, the burners do not produce an even flame from all the ga.s openings.
Of the following, the BEST thing to tell the tenant FIRST is that she should

   A. scrape off the caked-on drippings and then poke open all the clogged openings so the gas. will burn evenly
   B. remove the soiled parts of the burner and soak them in hot water with a mild cleaner to remove the dirt
   C. learn how to use the stove properly so that her food does not boil over or splatter onto the grids
   D. stop using the range until someone from the management office comes to adjust the flame

32.____

33. While inspecting a tenant's apartment, one of the things you should check is the drainage of the sinks. In testing the kitchen sink, you observe that there are coffee grinds and a film of grease in the drain basket.
Of the following, the BEST instructions to give the tenant are to

   A. throw coffee grinds in the garbage and wash oils down the drain
   B. collect oil in a can and put it in the garbage, but wash coffee grinds down with cold water
   C. avoid clogging, wash both coffee grinds and oil down the sink with hot, soapy water
   D. collect and dispose of coffee grinds and oils by putting them in the garbage and not in the sink

33.____

34. Mrs. Mary Jones and her family live in a 5-room apartment in a building on an urban renewal site. A public housing development is planned for this site. You are interviewing her with regard to relocation. During the interview, you learn that Mrs. Jones is divorced, unemployed, and receiving public assistance. Her four children are all under eight years of age, she is from a. small town in North Carolina, and she has lived in the city for over 2 1/2 years.
From 'your questions, what should you *immediately* know regarding relocation possibilities?
She is

   A. *eligible* for high priority in a public housing development
   B. *eligible* for public housing but not for another two months
   C. *not eligible* for public housing
   D. *not eligible* for public housing for another six months

34.____

35. You are about to visit a tenant to encourage him to move from the site when a neighbor tells you that for the last week the tenant has been quarreling loudly and constantly with his wife and children. When you knock on his door, he tells you to go away. You try several times to visit this apartment, but with no success.
What is the BEST thing to do in an effort to solve this problem?

35.____

A. Ask the neighbor to encourage him to let you in since he probably has confidence in the neighbor
B. Report the problem to your supervisor since the services of a social worker may be needed
C. Leave a note in the door telling the tenant to come to the site office
D. Call the police and tell them of the unusual difficulty you are having with this man

36. Which one of the following is the BEST kind of evidence presented by a tenant to prove that he actually lives at his current address?

    A. change-of-address form that the tenant has filled out for a creditor
    B. letter with the tenant's name and present address on it
    C. library card
    D. receipt

37. As an assistant, you could be asked to make a recommendation regarding the type of lighting fixtures a tenant should use.
    If you were concerned with not overburdening the present electrical circuits, a recommendation to use fluorescent lights rather than incandescent lights would be

    A. *good,* because fluorescent lights flicker less than , incandescent bulbs
    B. *good,* because fluorescent lights draw less current than incandescent bulbs
    C. *poor,* because fluorescent lights are very hard to install in a system designed for incandescent lights
    D. *poor,* because incandescent lights use less current than fluorescent lights

38. If a tenant had to move more than one time, moving expenses would be paid for all of the following combinations of moves EXCEPT

    A. an intrasite move and a subsequent move to a tenant-found apartment
    B. a move to another site and a subsequent move to public housing
    C. two moves to another site and a subsequent move to a tenant-found apartment
    D. a move-out to a tenant-found apartment and a subsequent move to public housing

39. The step of eviction of an on-site tenant is *generally* considered

    A. when a tenant has failed to pay a month's rent
    B. only when a tenant has refused to move into public housing
    C. as a last step in solving any housing problems of a tenant
    D. as a warning to an on-site tenant who is allowing more relatives to live with him than is noted on the S.O.R. card

40. Suppose that a tenant tells you her moving expenses will come to more than the amount she is eligible to receive. You WOULD tell her to

    A. pay the extra expense herself
    B. ask the Social Service Department for help
    C. submit a moving bill from the mover
    D. leave behind all broken furniture

KEY (CORRECT ANSWERS)

1. C	11. D	21. D	31. A
2. B	12. C	22. C	32. B
3. D	13. C	23. C	33. D
4. C	14. A	24. D	34. A
5. D	15. D	25. B	35. B
6. A	16. B	26. B	36. D
7. C	17. C	27. A	37. B
8. C	18. C	28. C	38. D
9. A	19. D	29. C	39. C
10. C	20. B	30. A	40. C

TEST 2

DIRECTIONS: Each question or incomplete statement is followed by several suggested answers or completions. Select the one that BEST answers the question or completes the statement. *PRINT THE LETTER OF THE CORRECT ANSWER IN THE SPACE AT THE RIGHT.*

1. Housing officials and experts have long suggested changing slum tenements into cooperatives.
   The PROBABLE reason that the advocates of tenement cooperatives feel that tenant-owners would be more likely than absentee landlords to keep buildings in good condition is that

   A. the tenant-owners would be living there while an absentee landlord would not
   B. the tenants in cooperatives want to demonstrate the advantages of cooperative living
   C. absentee landlords do not understand inner city problems
   D. absentee landlords have no reason to provide good maintenance

   1.____

2. A three-part plan to control the loss of an estimated sixty million dollars a year in welfare monies has been proposed.
   Which one of the following proposals would LEAST likely be part of this plan?

   A. Identification cards with photographs of the welfare client
   B. Face-to-face interviews with the welfare clients
   C. Computerized processing of welfare money records
   D. Individual cash payments to each member of a family

   2.____

3. Which one of the following statements describes the purpose of the Equal Rights Amendment which was passed by Congress but was not ratified by the required number of states?
   To

   A. eliminate state-enforced racial discrimination in public schools through extensive use of busing
   B. guarantee to aliens living in the United States the right to hold Civil Service jobs
   C. prohibit sex discrimination by any law or action of the government
   D. extend the right to vote to those previously ineligible by requiring only thirty days residency in a state

   3.____

4. In dealing with members of different ethnic groups in the area he serves, the assistant should give

   A. individuals the services required by his agency
   B. less service to those he judges to be more advantaged
   C. better service to groups with which he sympathizes most
   D. better service to groups with political *muscle*

   4.____

5. The MAJOR reason for joining a professional group such as The National Association of Housing and Redevelopment Officials, The Citizens Housing and Planning Council, or The National Housing Conference is to

   5.____

44

A. keep yourself informed about current ideas and
B. directions in the housing field · put it on your resume
C. get promoted
D. gain respect from fellow workers

6. Suppose you are interviewing a tenant whose clothing is sloppy, strange, or out of fashion.
Which of the following is MOST certain to be an appropriate action taken toward this tenant?

   A. Tell him he will get better service when he dresses better.
   B. Refer him to the Department of Social Services for help.
   C. Refer his children to the Bureau of Child Welfare.
   D. Treat him as respectfully as you treat other tenants.

6._____

7. An assistant may initiate an order that a tenant's welfare check be *rent-restricted* if that tenant has mismanaged his welfare check and not paid his rent.
Taking this action assures that

   A. all of the tenant's next welfare checks will be sent to the Urban Renewal Site as payment on account
   B. the Urban Renewal Site will receive a certain portion of the tenant's next welfare check and the tenant will receive the remainder
   C. the welfare center will send the Urban Renewal Site full payment for the rent and will require that the tenant repay this amount
   D. the welfare center will hold payment of checks from the tenant until they are notified by the assistant that the rent has been paid

7._____

8. For six months, a family lived in a 4-room apartment where they paid $376 a month. They made an intrasite move to a 4-room apartment where they paid $92 per room a month for six months.
Comparing the two six-month periods, the TOTAL amount of money the family saved by making the intrasite move was

   A. $48   B. $58   C. $86   D. $118

8._____

9. To calculate a tenant's usable income, you should make tax deductions of 4.4 percent on salary up to a maximum of $9,000 and state disability deductions of .5 percent on salary up to $3,000.
What does a tenant's COMBINED deduction amount to if his annual salary is $6,700?

   A. $228.00   B. $284.30   C. $309.80   D. $350.00

9._____

10. If the temporary relocation expenses for housing are set at $27 per day for one adult and $15 per day for each additional person in a room, how much money is allowed for a woman and four children temporarily relocated in one room for a period of six days?

    A. $252   B. $522   C. $567   D. $777

10._____

11. According to relocation policy, a family relocating to private housing from federally-aided or certain other sites will be granted a relocation payment. This payment equals the difference between 1/5 of the family's yearly income and the scheduled yearly rent for a standard apartment for their size family.
    Suppose a two-person family whose yearly income is $6,450 has been unable to obtain public housing and so finds a one-bedroom private apartment. The scheduled rent for a one-bedroom apartment appropriate for their occupancy is $120 a month. What payment will they receive?

    A. $120   B. $144   C. $150   D. $205

11.____

12. A family on a housing relocation site is paying $240 per month for rent. This represents 25% of their gross monthly income.
    If the husband earns 4/5 of their total combined monthly income, how much does the WIFE earn per month?

    A. $192   B. $324   C. $768   D. $960

12.____

13. In a nearly vacant building, there are only a few tenants left who are waiting to move into public housing. When you visit them to check their present conditions, you notice that some of the *tinned-up* apartments have the sheet metal partly pulled off the doors. The tenants tell you that they think that the many men who come and go frequently are drug addicts.
    The BEST action for you to take is to

    A. ignore the incident since all tenants will be moving out soon
    B. visit the site when you think someone might actually be selling drugs
    C. put up a sign warning these men that the building will be knocked down shortly
    D. report all your observations and the reports of the tenants to your supervisor

13.____

Questions 14-19.

DIRECTIONS: Answer Questions 14 through 19 on the basis of the information given in the passage below.

The City of X has set up a Maximum Base Rent Program for all rent-controlled apartments. The objective is to insure that the landlord will get a fair, but not excessive, profit on his building to stem the great tide of buildings being abandoned by their owners and to encourage landlords to continue the upkeep of their property. The Maximum Base Rent Program permits the landlord to raise rents under carefully devised standards, while practically no raises in rents in this City were permitted under previous guidelines.

Under this plan, the City determines a Maximum Ease Rent amount by means of a formula which takes into account the age of the building, the number of apartments, total rents received from the building, the amount of expenses, and labor costs. The Maximum Base Rent amount is to be recomputed every two years to allow for increases or decreases in building costs.

The Maximum Base Rent, which will allow the landlord to make a "fair return" on his investment, may not be collected immediately, however, since no rent increases over 7.5 percent will be permitted in any one year. The highest actual rent for each apartment during a given year will be called the Maximum Collectible Rent. This will be computed so that the increase over the present rent is not more . than 7.5 percent ($7.50 on every $100.00). Sometimes it may be less. Therefore, collectible rents will increase each year until the Maximum Base Rent is reached.

14. According to the above passage, the Maximum Base Rent is determined by the

    A. landlord
    B. Mayor
    C. Rent Commissioner
    D. City

15. Which of the following, according to the passage, permits a *fair return* on the landlord's investment?
    The _____ Rent Program.

    A. Minimum Base
    B. Maximum Base
    C. Minimum Collectible
    D. Maximum Collectible

16. It may be concluded from the passage that the City of X hopes that insuring fair profits for landlords will be followed by

    A. good upkeep of apartment buildings
    B. decreased interest rates on home mortgages
    C. lower rents in the future
    D. a better formula for determining rents

17. According to the passage, guidelines for determining rents previous to the Maximum Base Rent Program resulted in

    A. practically no raises in rents being made
    B. rent increases of approximately 10 percent a year
    C. a *fair return* to landlords from most rents
    D. landlords making too much money on their property

18. Based on the above passage, which is the MOST correct description of the kinds of facts that are taken into consideration when determining the Maximum Base Rent? Facts about

    A. labor costs and politics
    B. the landlord and labor costs
    C. the building and labor costs
    D. the building and the landlord

19. According to the above passage, the MAXIMUM annual increase in rent for a tenant in rent-controlled housing under the Maximum Base Rent Program is

    A. 7.5 percent each year for ten years
    B. 7.5 percent each year until the Maximum Base Rent is reached
    C. always under 7.5 percent a year
    D. $7.50 each year until it reaches $100.00

Questions 20-25.

DIRECTIONS: Answer Questions 20 through 25 on the basis of the information in the following form.

METROPOLITAN CITY

Last Name	First Name	Middle Initial
Smith	John	G.

Street		Apartment
758 Reason Street		1C

Borough or Town	State	Zip Code
Bronx	New York	10403

Monthly Rent	Number of Rooms	
$110.00	5	

E.

FAMILY COMPOSITION

	Name	Relation to Head	Birth Date Mo./Yr.	Annual Income	Employer or School
1.	Smith, John G.	Head	7/58	$10,400	Harris Chemical
2.	Smith, Ethel S.	Wife	3/61	0	
3.	Smith, Lucy M.	Daughter	4/81	0	P.S. 172
4.	Smith, John G., Jr.	Son	8/83	0	P.S. 172
5.	Smith, Susan F.	Daughter	1/88	0	
6.	Simmons, Sylvia T.	Mother-in-law	4/40	$4,680	F.W. Woolworth (part-time)
7.					

Total Annual Income	$15,080
Total Assets: Small Savings Accounts. Mr. Smith.	$5,000 life insurance on
Additional Information	

6 (#2)

20. The occupants of the Smith apartment are Mr. Smith, Mrs. Smith, ____ mother, their ____ and ____.   20.____

   A. her; son; daughters
   B. his; son; daughters
   C. her; sons; daughter
   D. her; sons; daughters

21. The income of the Smith household comes from the earnings of the father, the   21.____

   A. mother, the mother-in-law, and the children
   B. mother, and the children, but not the mother-in-law
   C. mother-in-law, and the children, but not the mother
   D. mother-in-law, but not the mother and children

22. From the information given about the Smith family, their apartment seems to be   22.____

   A. too small
   B. the right size
   C. a little large
   D. much too large

23. If an assistant goes to the Smiths' apartment to discuss their relocation and everyone is home except Mr. Smith, with whom should the assistant talk about relocation?   23.____

   A. John Jr. and Ethel Smith
   B. Ethel Smith and Sylvia Simmons
   C. Lucy and Ethel Smith
   D. John Smith, Jr. and Sylvia Simmons

24. The reason why the last column was left blank for Susan Smith is PROBABLY that   24.____

   A. the assistant forgot to ask for this information
   B. Susan's parents would not give this information
   C. Susan is too young to go to school
   D. Susan does not live at home

25. The section for Additional Information was left blank MOST probably because   25.____

   A. the assistant did not have time to ask for more information
   B. the Smith family is sufficiently well-described by the other information on the form
   C. the Additional Information section is not an important part of the form
   D. unfavorable facts have been purposely left out

26. Whenever a tenant moves into a private apartment for which a finder's fee is to be paid, this fee is payable to the   26.____

   A. landlord or broker
   B. tenant
   C. local site office
   D. Housing and Development Administration

27. When a relocated tenant moves into public housing in the city, all rents must be paid DIRECTLY to the   27.____

   A. Relocation and Management Services Office
   B. Housing and Redevelopment Administration

C. Model Cities Administration
D. City Housing Authority

28. According to relocation rules and regulations, in order for an apartment to be considered *standard*, it is LEAST important that the apartment

   A. not be overcrowded
   B. have a bathroom with a shower
   C. have hot and cold running water
   D. be free of hazardous violations

29. The PRIMARY purpose of the Finder's Fee Program is to

   A. provide a listing of private home owners willing to take in tenants during emergencies
   B. establish a link between private contractors and public housing
   C. arrange housing for those forced to vacate because of boiler breakdowns
   D. provide a listing of housing facilities in private housing

30. Which one of the following would MOST likely cause the GREATEST amount of damage to the asphalt tiles on apartment floors?

   A. Protective furniture casters
   B. Wet mopping
   C. Liquid wax
   D. Grease

31. The rents for three families in a relocation site come to a total of $0,720 per year. If Family A pays $3,480 per year and Family B pays $2,400 per year, how much does Family C pay?

   A. $2,760   B. $3,840   C. $4,200   D. $5,800

32. Of 180 families that relocated in a given month, one-fifth moved into Finder's Fee apartments, one-quarter moved into tenant-found apartments, one-third moved into public housing, and the rest moved out of the city.
   How many moved out of the city?

   A. 36   B. 39   C. 45   D. 60

33. If a tenant earns $5,280 a year and his rent is 25% of his annual income, the amount of rent he pays each month is

   A. $110   B. $115   C. $120   D. $135

34. The word *recycling* has become a popular one as used by those who are concerned with saving the environment. This word USUALLY refers to an interest in

   A. using bicycles again instead of automobiles for transportation
   B. the chemical treatment of rain water for drinking purposes
   C. collecting used bottles, cans, and newspaper which will be sold, treated, and re-used
   D. reorganizing public transportation routes in the city so that noise and traffic will be reduced

35. Recent accusations of fraud involving FHA-insured mortgages in various American cities have brought to light the fact that   35.____

    A. blockbusting has become the favorite tactic of real estate brokers
    B. families with incomes of $16,000 - $20,000 have been prevented from obtaining mortgages
    C. homes bought through false credit ratings at inflated prices were quickly lost by low income owners
    D. the bad design of homes involved has helped pollute the urban environment

KEY (CORRECT ANSWERS)

1.	A	16.	A
2.	D	17.	A
3.	C	18.	C
4.	A	19.	B
5.	A	20.	A
6.	D	21.	D
7.	B	22.	A
8.	A	23.	B
9.	C	24.	C
10.	B	25.	B
11.	C	26.	A
12.	A	27.	D
13.	D	28.	B
14.	D	29.	D
15.	B	30.	D

31. B
32. B
33. A
34. C
35. C

EXAMINATION SECTION
TEST 1

DIRECTIONS: Each question or incomplete statement is followed by several suggested answers or completions. Select the one that BEST answers the question or completes the statement. *PRINT THE LETTER OF THE CORRECT ANSWER IN THE SPACE AT THE RIGHT.*

1. An Assistant Housing Manager has called a subordinate into his office in order to discuss the subordinate's failure to perform some task adequately. The subordinate, when criticized, accused the Assistant Manager of being prejudiced against him. If this is the first time that such an incident has occurred, it would be best for the manager to

   A. assure the subordinate that the facts upon which the criticism was based will be reviewed, since the subordinate feels so strongly about the matter
   B. insist that the subordinate listen to the criticism and that he make no comment on it unless he can do so in an objective manner
   C. listen to whatever the subordinate has to say and indicate the basis for the criticism
   D. terminate the interview immediately and suggest that the discussion be continued at some other time

   1.____

2. Faced with a subordinate who is excessively dependent upon his superior in arriving at decisions, the superior should

   A. arrange to have the subordinate transferred to work which will not involve decision making
   B. continue to assist him in making decisions while instilling a feeling of confidence in the subordinate
   C. direct the subordinate to make his own decisions in areas assigned to him
   D. reprimand the subordinate for failing to perform the job properly

   2.____

3. A supervisor has called one of his subordinates into his office to inform him of his service rating. During the interview, the supervisor has praised the subordinate for his good points and also criticized his shortcomings. The subordinate has agreed without discussion to every criticism leveled against him by the supervisor. It would now be best for the supervisor to

   A. get the employee to review his shortcomings and to suggest a plan for minimizing them, before terminating the interview
   B. suggest that the employee reserve any opinion on the criticisms until the service rating appeal period
   C. terminate the interview after having outlined all of the employee's shortcomings and points of merit
   D. terminate the interview after praising the employee's general receptiveness to criticism and emphasizing that past mistakes will not count against him in the coming year

   3.____

4. A report to be sent to another subdivision of the Housing Authority has been prepared by a competent subordinate, in the name of the supervisor. It would be best for the supervisor to

   A. check the report in detail since it bears his name
   B. have the report checked in detail by another competent subordinate
   C. review the report briefly to pick up any obvious errors or omissions
   D. send the report forward without reading it

5. In establishing a work schedule for the performance of a particular job, the one of the following which is of LEAST importance is the

   A. number of employees available for assignment
   B. time by which the job must be finished
   C. time required for each separate part of the total job
   D. time required under very difficult or adverse conditions

6. One of the chief responsibilities of the supervisor is to make sure that the work is completed on time. In order to achieve this aim, it would be desirable for the supervisor to

   A. assign one employee to each specific task
   B. delegate responsibility in accordance with the abilities and capacities of his subordinates
   C. help out by doing as much of the work himself as he can
   D. schedule the work and keep informed of its progress

7. Effective supervisors apply proper principles of human relations. Application of such principles has what kind of effect on the need for detailed rules and regulations covering every aspect of the job?

   A. has no effect upon it
   B. increases the need for it
   C. reduces the need for it
   D. supersedes rules and regulations

8. Of the following, the most important generally approved method of maintaining high morale in one's staff is to

   A. advise the staff that personal problems must be left at home
   B. employ a jocular manner in issuing such reprimands as are necessary
   C. keep the staff informed of new developments and policies of the Housing Authority
   D. praise employees whenever such praise is warranted and refrain from direct criticism of their faults

9. When you become aware that a Housing Assistant under your supervision has failed to follow the proper procedure in making apartment inspections and has concealed this failure, it would be best for you to

   A. discuss with him both the failure to follow the proper procedure and the reason for this concealment, with the aim of improving the relationship between superior and subordinate
   B. make no mention of the matter to the assistant, but watch him more closely in the future

C. inform the assistant that the proper apartment inspection procedure must be followed since a uniform procedure is necessary for effective project management
D. review the proper apartment inspection procedure with the assistant and reprimand him for having concealed his failure to follow it

10. "The project manager does not formulate Housing Authority policy, but is responsible for executing policy formulated by top management. He is the administrative person closest to the employee group carrying out actual operations."
On this basis, a chLief function of the manager is to

    A. dissuade employees from giving suggestions on translating policy into action
    B. interpret policy in a way which will respect the personal interests and needs of the employees
    C. recommend promotion of personnel to top management
    D. report work schedules, work delays and staff assignments to top management so all the facts are available for decision making

11. The one of the following which is NOT a principle of effective operation in an organization is the need to

    A. coordinate the work of different divisions
    B. delegate to subordinates as much authority as they can assume within the scope of their jobs
    C. provide sufficient overlapping of authority to insure coverage of all aspects of operation
    D. trace and isolate problems, obstructions and other difficulties

12. A supervisor is most likely to achieve increased production by setting

    A. high but attainable goals, and according high praise to those subordinates who reach the goals
    B. low goals, and according high praise to those subordinates who exceed the goals
    C. moderately high goals, raising them as the more efficient subordinates approach them
    D. very high goals, and pressing the subordinates to reach them

13. Of the following, the most practical method of acquainting new employees with the details of routine rules and regulations of the Housing Authority is to

    A. assign each new employee to an older employee for instruction and clarification of procedures
    B. discuss with each new employee the nature of such rules and regulations shortly after he begins work
    C. hold a conference with all new employees to inform them of the rules and regulations
    D. provide a manual of rules and regulations for each employee

14. The practice of supervisors making themselves available to subordinates in order to listen to and help solve the subordinates' personal (off the job) problems is regarded as

    A. a form of paternalism rejected by both management and labor
    B. inadvisable since supervisors are seldom equipped to do such counseling
    C. proper in the maintenance of good personal relations
    D. undesirable since it represents the intrusion into the subordinates' personal affairs

14.____

15. An important educational principle that should be recognized by supervisors who are training subordinates is that

    A. any effective method of instruction will work equally well with all subordinates in a given title
    B. individual instruction is the only reliable method of training the average individual
    C. interested and capable persons will learn at different rates of speed when taking the same course of training
    D. people over 60 years of age have little capacity for learning

15.____

16. Assume that a Housing Manager disagrees with a new policy which has just been adopted by the central office. When he explains to his staff the policy and its application, there are criticisms and objections, many of which reflect his own point of view. It would be best for the manager to

    A. agree that the policy is defective but direct that it must be carried out
    B. explain the basis for the policy and order the staff to follow it
    C. modify the policy to meet the most valid objections to insure willing compliance with the policy
    D. refute the criticisms and objections regardless of his own opinion in the matter

16.____

17. A staff conference has been called by a supervisor for the purpose of considering means which may be used to solve a particular problem. In this situation, it is most important for the supervisor to

    A. encourage discussion, but discourage argument
    B. express his own views and opinions first
    C. permit the discussion to continue until everyone attending the conference is satisfied he has had his full say
    D. remain impartial, indicating neither approval or disapproval of any suggestions which may be presented

17.____

18. At staff meetings a manager is faced with a subordinate who takes every opportunity to make comments and gripe about one particular procedure. It would be best for the manager to

    A. assert his authority and warn the griper that publicly aired complaints will not be tolerated
    B. briefly explain management's reason for the procedure griped about
    C. ignore the gripes
    D. tell the griper that the problem at hand is how best to operate under the established procedure

18.____

19. One member of the staff, at staff meetings, likes to argue frequently and at length. It would be best for the supervisor to

    A. exclude him from staff meetings
    B. hear his arguments and answer them briefly
    C. talk to him privately and enlist his help in reducing arguments at staff meetings
    D. talk to other members of the staff, requesting that they not become involved in arguments with the offending member

19.____

20. At a staff conference conducted by you, there are frequent interruptions of the general discussion which indicate lack of understanding of the objectives of the conference. Of the following, the most reasonable conclusion to draw from this situation is that

    A. adequate control over the trend of the discussion was lacking
    B. conferees were probably antagonistic to the objectives of the conference
    C. content of the discussion bore little relation to the actual work assignments of the conferees
    D. objectives of the conference may not have been clearly expressed at the start of the conference

20.____

21. One of the staff members at a project frequently has good ideas but expresses them poorly when presenting them at staff meetings. It would be best for the manager to

    A. accept the ideas as they are presented, without commenting on the method of expression
    B. allow the staff member to state his ideas and for the manager to paraphrase them so they are easily understood
    C. defer consideration of the ideas until the next staff meeting so that the staff member can have time to put them in clearer form
    D. suggest to the staff member that he inform the manager of his ideas before the meeting so that the manager can rephrase them and present them so that they are more easily understood

21.____

22. In the course of several interviews with a certain tenant, you notice several incidents of peculiar behavior on the part of her child whom she has brought along with her to the office. The behavior appears to indicate an emotional disturbance requiring psychiatric help. The most advisable course of action for you to follow is to

    A. bring the situation to the attention of a child guidance clinic so that they may take appropriate action
    B. discuss the situation with the mother in an attempt to make her aware of the problem and the possible need for treatment
    C. tactfully point out to the mother that the child is emotionally disturbed and should be treated by a psychiatrist
    D. take no action on the situation but make a note of it in the tenant folder

22.____

23. An accepted concept of management of public housing is that it should "studiously avoid attitudes of paternalism." To avoid the paternalistic approach in dealing with tenants, management should

    A. deal with tenants as individuals rather than in organized groups
    B. emphasize its interest in good tenant relations, but avoid making specific recommendations on problems brought to it by tenants

23.____

C. emphasize objective uniform procedures in dealing with tenant problems
D. not interest itself in an unemployment problem brought to its attention by a tenant

24. Housing management should realize that the most essential factor contributing to the success of a community activities program is

A. adequacy of facilities
B. availability of funds
C. existence of a sponsoring agency
D. quality of leadership in activities

25. The one of the following which LEAST characterizes the dealings of the Housing Authority with agencies sponsoring community activities programs in projects is that the Authority

A. gives certain forms of financial assistance
B. permits retention of agency identity
C. provides government direction
D. requires reports on activities and progress

KEY (CORRECT ANSWERS)

1. C	11. C
2. B	12. A
3. A	13. D
4. C	14. C
5. D	15. C
6. D	16. B
7. C	17. A
8. C	18. D
9. A	19. C
10. B	20. D

21. B
22. B
23. C
24. D
25. C

TEST 2

DIRECTIONS: Each question or incomplete statement is followed by several suggested answers or completions. Select the one that BEST answers the question or completes the statement. *PRINT THE LETTER OF THE CORRECT ANSWER IN THE SPACE AT THE RIGHT.*

1. The one of the following which best indicates the extent to which teenage boys and girls may be permitted to plan their own leisure-time activities program is:　　1.____

    A. Give the teenagers full responsibility for planning
    B. Leave the planning in the hands of the community activities coordinator or other professional leadership
    C. Permit certain selected teenagers to offer suggestions on planning, but leave all decisions up to the community activities coordinator
    D. Provide for joint responsibility of teenagers and professional leadership in planning

2. A frequent criticism of the construction of public housing developments in slum areas has been the　　2.____

    A. failure to consider the transportation needs of tenants
    B. failure to modify in any way the established gridiron pattern of slum thoroughfares
    C. failure to reduce population densities to desirable density standards
    D. lack of provision for slum site families in public housing developments

3. As part of a report to the central office, a graph is to be prepared to show the rental income of a housing project, the amount which has been spent on heating, and the amount which has been spent on maintenance, each year for a five-year period. The best type of graph to use is a　　3.____

    A. bar graph　　　　　　　　　　B. circle graph
    C. pictorial graph　　　　　　　D. proportional graph

4. Of the following arguments which may be used in an effort to urge residential site tenants to move, the LEAST suitable is to　　4.____

    A. assure displaced families that they will be given first preference in choice of apartments in the new project
    B. explain that new projects will provide wholesome housing quarters for many families
    C. indicate why a slum area is not a desirable place in which to live and raise a family
    D. point out that stores, movies and other similar services will soon go out of business to make room for the new project

5. The Housing Authority does not usually attempt to replace or make major improvements in the heating and plumbing systems of site buildings, even when such systems are somewhat defective or present operating difficulties. The chief reason for this policy is that　　5.____

    A. buildings on sites are of such a heterogeneous nature and generally so out-of-date that repair and replacement parts are unobtainable
    B. it is economically unsound to make major improvements in buildings which will soon be demolished

C. poor heating and plumbing services are very effective in encouraging tenants to move as quickly as possible
D. there is no need for the Authority to make repairs which the previous owner was unwilling to make

6. A site building has a coal-fired steam boiler as the heating plant. While using the boiler, proper examination of the water gauge fails to reveal the presence of any water. Of the following, it would be best that

    A. a small amount of water be let into the boiler immediately, increasing the amount of water gradually until the proper level is reached
    B. the fire be put out immediately by covering with sand
    C. the fire be put out immediately by spraying with warm water
    D. the required amount of water be put into the boiler immediately

6.____

7. The principal reason why a record is kept of "removable items" (so designated by the city's appraisers) which are left behind by commercial site tenants when they move out is that the

    A. award for moving expenses may be appropriately reduced
    B. commercial tenant may receive an award for the removable items
    C. items may be enumerated and taken into account in demolition contracts
    D. presence of the items will be known in the event they are reclassified as fixtures

7.____

8. When a commercial tenant, occupying space in a building purchased by the Housing Authority for demolition, moves prior to the date of condemnation, leaving behind certain fixtures, he is ordinarily entitled to

    A. a fixture award plus moving expenses
    B. a fixture award to be paid by the former owner as determined by the court at the time of condemnation
    C. no fixture award
    D. the same fixture award he would receive if he had waited until after the date of condemnation

8.____

9. To expedite the clearance of one site it may be necessary to transfer a residential tenant to a second site. In this event, the tenant is entitled, in so far as priority for admission to a project is concerned, to

    A. former site occupant status at the first site but no preference at the second site
    B. no former site occupant status but preference for admission to a project so long as he remains a site tenant
    C. site occupant status at the second site but no preference at the first site
    D. site tenant status at the second site and former site occupant status at the first site

9.____

10. Security deposits are required of all project tenants EXCEPT the following:

    A. recipients of assistance from the Department of Welfare
    B. resident employees
    C. resident employees and recipients of full assistance from the Department of Welfare
    D. resident employees and recipients of full Old Age Assistance

10.____

11. The most accurate statement concerning the eligibility for public housing of persons engaged in professional occupations, such as doctors, dentists or lawyers, is that they are

    A. eligible on the same basis as non-professionals
    B. eligible when engaged in their profession only part time, and if they meet the standards of eligibility, including income
    C. eligible when not self-employed, and if they meet the standards of eligibility, including income
    D. ineligible under all circumstances

11.____

12. A family group consisting of a husband, wife, son and an unrelated individual who has resided with them for 20 years applies for a project apartment. Considering family composition only, this family group is

    A. eligible for admission only to federally aided and city-aided projects
    B. eligible for admission only to state-aided and city-aided projects
    C. eligible for admission to all projects
    D. not eligible for public housing

12.____

13. A natural family group contains, in addition, one or more foster children for the support of whom the family receives remuneration from an accredited social agency. If the family meets other eligibility requirements, it is eligible for admission to

    A. all projects, the remuneration not to be considered income
    B. all projects, the remuneration not to be considered in determining eligibility, but to be considered in determining rent
    C. all projects, but, in the case of federally aided projects, the remuneration is to be considered income in determining rent and eligibility
    D. federally and city-aided projects only

13.____

14. The one of the following which is the most complete list of requirements for eligibility for an apartment in a public housing project for a single-person family is:

    A. 55 years of age or older; has been maintaining his own separate living quarters, or is a roomer in a hotel, rooming house or lodging house
    B. physically able to care for himself; able to maintain his apartment; 55 years of age or older; has been maintaining his own separate living quarters
    C. physically able to care for himself; 50 years of age or older; has been maintaining his own separate living quarters, or is a roomer in a hotel, rooming house or lodging house
    D. physically able to care for himself; 50 years of age or older

14.____

15. If a tenant who has been served with a notice of ineligibility, but not with a notice to vacate, moves from his apartment without notifying the Housing Authority prior to the date of move-out, he shall be charged rent

    A. for a period not to exceed seven days after the date of move-out, depending on the vacancy loss
    B. for a period not to exceed 15 days after the date of move-out, depending on the vacancy loss
    C. only through the date of move-out
    D. for the full calendar month, regardless of vacancy loss

15.____

16. As the population of cities increases, there is a decrease in the proportion of the developed urban land area which is used for 16.____

    A. commercial purposes
    B. industrial purposes
    C. parks and open areas
    D. residential purposes
    E. streets and thoroughfares

17. If valid criteria have been used in tenant selection for public housing projects, the result most likely to be attained is 17.____

    A. homogeneity of tenant characteristics will be assured
    B. larger Federal subsidies will be required
    C. neediest families will receive the greatest proportion of aid
    D. the underlying conditions of slums will be ameliorated
    E. management problems will be satisfied

18. On August 26 a tenant notifies the project of an increase in income which became effective on August 12. This increased income will require a rent increase for the tenant. His new increased rent becomes effective on the first of 18.____

    A. August   B. September   C. October   D. November

19. In calculating the anticipated income of a project tenant, the one of the following which shall NOT be included is 19.____

    A. unemployment insurance benefits
    B. veteran's mustering-out payments
    C. Workmen's Compensation payments
    D. Workmen's Compensation payments, when the employee also has income from other employment

20. An investigation has been made of a broken window pane in an apartment on the third floor which the tenant claims was broken by children playing outside. The investigation disclosed that there were several small holes in the window pane. Each hole is approximately cone-shaped and is about 3/16 inch in diameter on the inside of the glass (room side) and about 1/2 inch in diameter on the outside. Cracks connected some of these holes. On the basis of this information, the tenant should 20.____

    A. be charged for the window pane since the damage is not normal wear-and-tear and it is not possible to substantiate the tenant's claim
    B. be charged for the window pane since the nature of the damage indicates that it was caused from inside
    C. not be charged for the window pane since it is not possible to determine the cause of the damage and the low floor involved does not tend to support the tenant's explanation
    D. not be charged for the window pane since the nature of the damage indicates that it was caused from outside

21. Suppose you are studying the need for improving the effectiveness of operation of a particular activity. In making this study, you should pay LEAST attention to the

    A. amount of time which is consumed in this activity
    B. degree of prestige which will accrue to you
    C. number of persons engaged in this activity
    D. possible revision of employee work schedules
    E. value of the end product resulting from the activity

21.____

22. In training employees under your supervision, a basic fact to recognize is that

    A. instruction should be the same for all, since learning rates are uniform for all employees in a given title
    B. it is difficult to train persons above the age of 40 years
    C. persons differ in the amount they learn in a given period of time
    D. the training process should begin on a highly technical level if the subject matter to be learned is highly technical
    E. training can seldom achieve its purpose unless individual instruction is the method used

22.____

23. A group of newly appointed Housing Assistants has been assigned to your project. Of the following, the most important thing for you to do when they report for work on their first day is to

    A. acquaint them with the general features of the duties they are to perform
    B. allow them to ask questions freely about the conditions of work and the possibilities of advancement
    C. ascertain their sympathy with the social philosophy behind low-rent public housing
    D. distribute a schedule of visits to tenants to acquaint the Housing Assistants with the typical situations they will encounter
    E. inform them about time, sickness, absence and vacation regulations

23.____

24. Of the following, the best incentive to better work to employ in the supervision of a recently appointed Housing Assistant is, in general, to compare his present progress with

    A. previous progress made by him at the project
    B. progress of Housing Assistants of average ability at the project
    C. progress of the least competent Housing Assistant at the project
    D. progress of the most efficient Housing Assistant at the project
    E. progress of Housing Assistants in general at all projects

24.____

25. Of the following, the most important basis upon which to evaluate the efficiency of a subordinate is his

    A. accuracy and promptness in execution of assignments
    B. awareness of the social aspects of the assignments given to him
    C. confidence in the handling of difficult assignments
    D. observance of the rules and regulations of the Authority
    E. relationship with fellow employees

25.____

KEY (CORRECT ANSWERS)

1.	D	11.	C
2.	C	12.	C
3.	A	13.	A
4.	A	14.	C
5.	B	15.	C
6.	B	16.	D
7.	D	17.	C
8.	C	18.	C
9.	D	19.	B
10.	D	20.	B or C

21.	B
22.	C
23.	A
24.	A
25.	A

TEST 3

DIRECTIONS: Each question or incomplete statement is followed by several suggested answers or completions. Select the one that BEST answers the question or completes the statement. *PRINT THE LETTER OF THE CORRECT ANSWER IN THE SPACE AT THE RIGHT.*

1. A Housing Assistant under your supervision attempts to conceal the fact that he has made an error. Of the following, the most reasonable interpretation of this action is that the

    A. action of the Housing Assistant indicates an independent attitude
    B. desire for concealment of the error demonstrates an antisocial attitude
    C. error was probably a minor one which the Housing Assistant felt did not have to be reported to superior authority
    D. evasion indicates the possibility of an inadequate relationship between you and the Housing Assistant
    E. Housing Assistant does not know the proper procedure to follow

1.____

2. A Housing Assistant under your supervision complains that he deserves a higher service rating than the one he received recently. Your review of his work indicates that his work performance was average and that the standard rating he received was a just rating. Of the following, the most appropriate reply to his complaint is to

    A. advise him that he may appeal to the Civil Service Commission for a higher rating
    B. point out the below-average aspects of his work which were not included in his service rating report
    C. tell him not to be too concerned about his rating since he was considered a satisfactory employee
    D. tell him that the Departmental Personnel Board, and not you, is responsible for the allocation of service ratings
    E. tell him why his work was considered average and did not deserve more than a standard rating

2.____

3. A subject which is LEAST desirable as a topic in group discussion of interviewing problems is

    A. effect of the setting of an interview on the success of the interview
    B. evaluation of the interviews handled by the least efficient staff member
    C. handling language difficulties at interviews
    D. maximum utilization of application forms on which interviews are based
    E. subjective attitudes of applicants for low-rent public housing

3.____

4. A Housing Assistant criticizes a form which has been used in connection with applications for low-rent housing as poor because it limits the interviewer to specified areas of discussion with applicants. Of the following, the most appropriate course of action for you, as his supervisor, to take is to

    A. ascertain the need for further guidance of this Housing Assistant by reviewing his past use of this form
    B. ask the Housing Assistant to explain the limitations of the form in relation to required job performance

4.____

C. make a study of records of interviews by other Housing Assistants to determine the validity of the criticism
D. tell the Housing Assistant that such limitation is necessary to avoid interviews of undue length
E. tell the Housing Assistant that the ability of an employee to adhere to the form in his interviews is related to his understanding of standard procedures

5. One of your Housing Assistants has shown himself to be inaccurate in checking tenant income records. The action most likely to result in improvement in the work habits of this employee is to

   A. assign him to work that will not require close attention to details
   B. have him study a group of tenant income records which have been accurately checked
   C. review with him some of the records he has checked
   D. tell him that it is just as easy to do his job the right way
   E. warn that he will receive an unsatisfactory rating if he persists in being careless

6. Assume that a new procedure of interviewing has been adopted by the management division which you think may meet with some staff resistance. To reduce such possible resistance to a minimum, the best of the following steps to take is to

   A. advise the staff that they will have to accept the new procedure regardless of their personal feelings about it
   B. appoint a staff committee to study the procedure and report on its objectionable and desirable features
   C. ask staff members who in the past have been resistant to new procedures to comment on the new procedure before it is effective
   D. hold a staff meeting to discuss the meaning and application of the procedure prior to the date it is effective
   E. issue detailed instructions on the use of the new procedure to facilitate its application

7. To determine if assignments made to employees under your supervision are being carried out, the most practical supervisory method is to

   A. develop work-flow charts for use in checking work performance
   B. establish production quotas and work schedules
   C. evaluate periodic reports of work performed by subordinates
   D. give detailed instructions for all work assignments and delegate authority for work performance
   E. keep subordinates under constant surveillance to see that details of assignments are executed properly

8. "Samples of income re-examination records of Housing Assistants, in which no change in income or eligibility is involved, should be reviewed periodically." Of the following, the LEAST important reason for such periodic review is to

   A. correct errors in the application of re-examination procedures
   B. indicate a basis for efficiency ratings of these employees
   C. insure uniformity in application of re-examination procedures

D. obtain data as to the need for further training of Housing Assistants in eligibility review procedures
E. provide a means of determining the comparative production of each Housing Assistant

9. Suppose that a study is to be made of the adequacy of work schedules for maintenance personnel at your project. Of the following, the best first step to take is to

    A. arrange for detailed surveys of actual performance to obtain needed data
    B. discuss current work schedules with the building superintendent and his assistant superintendents
    C. have each employee submit a statement of his daily tasks and the time required for each task
    D. review typical work schedules of other projects to provide the basis for desired standards of work output
    E. utilize records of complaints as to service and breakdown of equipment as the starting point of the study

10. Of the following, the most important reason for planning work schedules for subordinates is that

    A. coverage of essential operations is more likely to be maintained
    B. emergency situations can be handled more expeditiously
    C. subordinates are more likely to be satisfied with their assignments if routinized
    D. supervisory relationships will be clarified and strengthened
    E. the basis for most tenant complaints will be eliminated

11. An employee under your supervision has shown difficulty in organizing his work. Consequently, the quality and quantity of his work output has been below acceptable standards. Of the following, the most effective way of improving the performance of this employee is to

    A. advise the employee to set up a tickler system so that he will not forget essential tasks
    B. encourage the employee to organize his work more efficiently
    C. explain the relationship of proper organization of work to work output
    D. help the employee discover the factors that may be hindering effective organization of work
    E. lay out the work of the employee until he is able to organize his work properly by himself

12. Suppose you have been assigned as site manager of a newly acquired slum clearance site. Of the following, the first major task you should undertake is to

    A. approach community agencies to solicit aid in tenant relocation
    B. establish criteria for determination of usability of residential buildings for which demolition may be deferred
    C. establish procedures for the acceptance from site tenants of applications for permanent low-rent housing
    D. establish reasonable time limits for removal of tenants from the site
    E. plan and administer a complete tenant and physical inventory

13. While walking down the steps of one of the project buildings, you notice a porter doing his work very poorly. Of the following, the proper action for you to take is to

    A. advise the building superintendent that the porter did not seem to know how to do his work
    B. analyze the porter's record to determine if it is satisfactory
    C. inform the building superintendent that a training program for porters appears advisable
    D. question the porter to ascertain whether he knows the proper way to do the job
    E. tell the porter that he is delinquent in his duties

14. After an accident has occurred and the injured employee has been given needed care, it is accepted practice to make a thorough determination of the cause of the accident. From the viewpoint of management, the most important purpose of such accident investigations is to

    A. establish the extent of liability of management in each case
    B. indicate to maintenance employees their responsibility in accident prevention
    C. maintain the morale of the staff and tenants
    D. obtain the necessary data for the liability insurer
    E. prevent the recurrence of such accidents

15. When a congested urban slum area is given over to a private or public housing project, the setting aside, at the same time, of additional space for school building is

    A. undesirable because it tends to decrease the amount of tax-producing property and thereby increase the tax burden on other property owners
    B. undesirable because the location of a school building depends on other additional factors which can be better determined at a later date
    C. desirable because property owners in the area raise fewer objections when land is condemned for both project and school at the same time
    D. desirable because suitable land may otherwise not be readily available for this purpose
    E. desirable because a school is an essential part of the community

16. The most important reason why Housing Assistants should be acquainted with the significant social foci of the housing project neighborhood is that

    A. a more constructive approach for the improvement of intra-family relations may be obtained
    B. better relations between project families and neighborhood families may be fostered
    C. fewer referrals to social agencies will need to be made
    D. neighborhood needs may be assessed more adequately
    E. tenants may be better advised how to budget their incomes

17. The most important positive result of tenant organization from the viewpoint of management is that it

    A. acts as a control on the possible slipshod work of subordinate members of the staff
    B. enables management to avoid complaints of an individual nature
    C. inevitably serves as a filter through which only important tenant problems affecting general welfare pass on to management

D. provides a means for bringing problems to the surface which otherwise might not be known or understood by management
E. usually engages the interests of tenants who will assume positions of leadership in the community

18. Where imminence of eviction of an applicant makes it impracticable to schedule a housing investigation, it is essential that prior to acceptance as an emergency applicant in a permanent project, he submit

   A. conclusive proof of residence at the address from which he is being evicted
   B. detailed proof of income eligibility
   C. evidence that he is unable to find suitable quarters pending completion of the housing investigation
   D. primary proof of citizenship
   E. proof that he is financially responsible or is a recipient of public assistance

19. When the building superintendent tells you that the transformer of one of the oil burners is defective, he is referring to the device which

   A. atomizes the liquid oil prior to ignition
   B. changes low-pressure steam to high-pressure steam
   C. increases the voltage for oil ignition
   D. regulates oil temperature prior to atomization
   E. supplies the proper voltage for operation of the motor

20. When a building superintendent reports corroded flashings resulting in leakage, the part of the building he is referring to is the

   A. basement piping
   B. boiler room
   C. pavement adjoining building
   D. roof
   E. stair halls

21. If an automatic elevator is not leveling properly at floor stops, the proper action to take is to

   A. allow the car to remain in service only if the distance between the car floor and floor landing is 3 inches or less
   B. post signs in the elevator to warn passengers
   C. station a maintenance man near the ground floor stop to warn passengers
   D. take the car out of service during slow periods to make necessary adjustments
   E. take the car out of service immediately to make necessary adjustments

22. Although rock salt is commonly used on the walks of the project when they are iced or heavily packed with snow, the chief disadvantage of its use is that it

   A. creates a very slushy condition
   B. generally causes deterioration of concrete walks
   C. increases cleaning costs if used intensively
   D. is harmful to adjacent trees and shrubs
   E. tends to increase the accident hazard

23. When instructing tenants how to clean enamel-painted woodwork, the tenant should be advised to wash the surfaces with 23.____

    A. ammonia water
    B. mild soap and water solution
    C. plain warm water
    D. strong soda solution
    E. vinegar and water solution

24. Of the following items included in the work schedule of porters, the one that should be assigned as a daily duty is 24.____

    A. cleaning incinerators
    B. cleaning stairhall windows and woodwork
    C. mopping all assigned stairhalls
    D. sweeping all stair landings
    E. washing down all sidewalks adjacent to assigned buildings

25. Some housing projects have, in the past, reduced their personnel cost for community activities by using tenant volunteers. The major disadvantage of this practice is that 25.____

    A. volunteers have no financial ties to oblige them to carry on the work regularly and efficiently
    B. tenant volunteers may not be aware of the most desirable methods of group work
    C. tenant volunteers are usually unable to obtain the respect and cooperation of fellow tenants
    D. demands of tenants for further participation in management operation will be fostered
    E. antagonism between tenant volunteers and tenants using community facilities is a general occurrence

26. "Studies in the cities of Hartford, Chicago, Philadelphia, Newark and New York showed that the rate of juvenile delinquency was highest in areas where housing was least adequate." 26.____
    On the basis of this quotation, it is most correct to say that

    A. no relationship can be established at all since bad housing is but one factor among many that may cause delinquent behavior
    B. areas of substandard housing are generally areas of high juvenile delinquency
    C. provision of adequate housing is probably the most effective tool in combating juvenile delinquency
    D. slum areas are less effectively policed than other areas in the cities mentioned
    E. the physical aspects of housing have direct causal relationship with the rate of juvenile delinquency

In questions 27 through 30, each paragraph contains five words in **bold** type, one of which is not in keeping with the meaning of the selection. In the space provided, write the letter of the one of the five words given that does not belong as written in the statement.

27. "The **minimum** amount that can be paid by the **Federal** government in any year as annual **contributions** to a low-rent housing project under a given contract of financial aid is a **fixed** percentage of the total **development** cost of the project."

    A. minimum   B. Federal   C. contributions   D. fixed
    E. development

27.____

28. "The existence and **dimensions** of the slums had long been **recognized** by State legislatures and municipalities, but these local public bodies and officers had **wasted** their efforts primarily on **unintegrated** remedial measures **restricted** in character to building and health codes."

    A. dimensions   B. recognized   C. wasted   D. unintegrated
    E. restricted

28.____

29. "One of the **major** purposes of a program of land **assembly** for urban redevelopment is to direct the location of new **home** building to **zoned** city land by erasing the margin that seems to favor unused **fringe** land."

    A. major   B. assembly   C. home   D. zoned
    E. fringe

29.____

30. Migration of **non-farm** families is estimated to **increase** the needs for housing construction only to the extent that **out-migration** from individual localities is so great as to leave an actual **deficit** of standard housing in those localities **after** demolition of all sub-standard units."

    A. non-farm   B. increase   C. out-migration   D. deficit
    E. after

30.____

KEY (CORRECT ANSWERS)

1.	D	16.	B
2.	E	17.	D
3.	B	18.	A
4.	B	19.	C
5.	C	20.	D
6.	D	21.	E
7.	C	22.	D
8.	E	23.	B
9.	B	24.	D
10.	A	25.	A
11.	D	26.	B
12.	E	27.	A
13.	A	28.	C
14.	E	29.	D
15.	D	30.	D

EXAMINATION SECTION
TEST 1

DIRECTIONS: Each question or incomplete statement is followed by several suggested answers or completions. Select the one that BEST answers the question or completes the statement. *PRINT THE LETTER OF THE CORRECT ANSWER IN THE SPACE AT THE RIGHT.*

1. The Model Cities program, which was authorized by the *Demonstration Cities and Metropolitan Development Act* was designed to

    A. help selected areas plan, administer, and carry out coordinated physical and social programs to improve the environment
    B. aid non-profit organizations to develop and demonstrate new ways of providing housing for low-income families
    C. encourage architects and builders to devise new large-scale construction techniques
    D. offer an alternative to usual urban renewal procedures through funding specific renewal activities on a yearly basis

1._____

2. The MAJOR purpose of the capital budgeting process in local government is to

    A. provide operating funds for the various departments
    B. centralize budget decision power in the executive branch
    C. centralize budget decision power in the Council
    D. establish a rational system of priorities for construction

2._____

3. The economic base of a community is

    A. the number of wealthy people with annual earnings in excess of $100,000 per year as a ratio to the total population
    B. the percentage of factory employed residents as a ratio of the total work force
    C. the productive industries located within the boundaries of a community
    D. those activities which provide the basic employment and income on which the rest of the local economy depends

3._____

4. One of the reasons for the creation of *superagencies* within city government was to

    A. create agencies that would serve as liaisons between the mayor's office and the community
    B. decentralize some of the functions for which the old agencies formerly had responsibility
    C. make each agency autonomous
    D. eliminate duplication of activities among different agencies

4._____

5. The word *autonomy* means

    A. automatic
    B. disregard of externals
    C. unlimited power or authority
    D. independent, self-governing

5._____

6. De facto, as in de facto segregation, means

   A. by right, in accordance with law
   B. actual
   C. disguised
   D. unintentional

7. American cities gain their legal powers from

   A. the Federal government
   B. the State government
   C. the United States Constitution
   D. common law

8. In an average urban area, the one of the following land uses that would account for the LARGEST percentage of land is

   A. residences
   B. streets
   C. business and industry
   D. public and semi-public uses

9. A cul-de-sac street is a

   A. dead-end street terminating in a circular turn-around
   B. loop street branching off from a collector street
   C. narrow street which has become congested as the result of commercial development
   D. gridiron street on which through traffic is prohibited

10. In the city, the capital budget is initially prepared by the

    A. city council
    B. comptroller
    C. city planning commission
    D. budget director

11. Reasonably well-to-do residential communities have joined the search for non-residential taxpayers but have shown LEAST inclination to plan for

    A. the necessary public utilities
    B. adequate access to the sites
    C. housing the workers
    D. the Budget Director

12. The GREATEST percentage of the daytime population of the business center of the city arrives by

    A. railroad
    B. subway
    C. bus
    D. passenger car

13. The LARGEST single public expenditure in most cities and suburbs in the State is for

    A. schools and education
    B. highways
    C. hospitals and health facilities
    D. police protection

14. The legal basis of zoning is 14.____

    A. the police power
    B. the power to levy taxes
    C. the Federal Constitution
    D. a special act of Congress

15. A drug used in addiction programs as a substitute for heroin is 15.____

    A. benzedrine   B. librium
    C. methadone   D. methanimine

16. The STOLcraft is a(n) 16.____

    A. high speed hydrofoil proposed as an alternative to the use of the ferry
    B. vehicle which travels just above the surface of either land or water on a cushion of air
    C. airplane intended for short distance trips between city centers
    D. cargo ship for containerized freight

Questions 17-21.

DIRECTIONS: Questions 17 through 21 are to be answered on the basis of the following information.

FLOOR AREA

Floor area is the sum of the gross areas of the several floors of a building or buildings, measured from the exterior faces of exterior walls or from the center lines of walls separating two buildings.

FLOOR AREA RATIO

Floor area ratio is the total floor area on a zoning lot, divided by the lot area of that zoning lot. (For example, a building containing 20,000 square feet of floor area on a zoning lot of 10,000 square feet has a floor area ratio of 2.0.) Expressed as a formula:

$$FAR = \frac{Floor\ Area}{Lot\ Area}$$

OPEN SPACE RATIO

The *open space ratio* of a zoning lot is the number of square feet of open space on the zoning lot, expressed as a percentage of the floor area on that zoning lot. (For example, if for a particular building an open space ratio of 20 is required, 20,000 square feet of floor area in the building would necessitate 4,000 square feet of open space on the zoning lot upon which the building stands, or, if 6,000 square feet of lot area were in open space, 30,000 square feet of floor area could be in the building on that zoning lot.) Each square foot of open space per 100 square feet of floor area is referred to as one point.

Expressed as a formula:

$$OSR = \frac{100 \times open\ space}{Floor\ Area}$$

17. If a building can be built with a maximum floor area ratio (FAR) of 10.0, this means   17.___

    A. the building can have a maximum of ten stories
    B. the maximum ratio of gross square feet of floor area to area of the first floor is 10:1
    C. that open space on the zoning lot must be provided in an amount equal to ten percent of the total floor area of the building
    D. the maximum ratio of gross square feet of floor area to lot area is 10:1

18. If the open space ratio of a particular building is 18.5 and the actual amount of open space is 13,550 square feet, the floor area of the building must be MOST NEARLY   18.___

    A. 250,675   B. 73,243   C. 28,170   D. 79,027

19. Given: A housing site of 43,560 square feet.   19.___
    At an FAR of 3.33, the allowable total floor area of a proposed building would be MOST NEARLY

    A. 30,736   B. 484,482   C. 48,448   D. 145,055

20. Given: A housing site of 43,560 square feet.   20.___
    At an FAR of 2.94 and an open space ratio of 24.0, how much open space must be provided?

    A. 30,736   B. 10,454   C. 14,816   D. 18,150

21. Given: A housing site of 43,560 square feet.   21.___
    If a proposed building on this site were to have 122,839 gross square feet of floor space, what would the FAR be?

    A. 10.0
    B. 25.5
    C. 2.82
    D. Cannot be determined from data given

Questions 22-24.

DIRECTIONS: Questions 22 through 24 are to be answered on the basis of the following table.

The age characteristics of the total population in a certain neighborhood are as follows:

Age	Number of People
3	2
5	4
12	3
18	3
20	1
21	3
22	4
50	2
56	1
72	2

22. The mean age of the population in the neighborhood described above is MOST NEARLY   22.____

    A. 15   B. 19   C. 23   D. 27

23. The median age of the population in the neighborhood described above is MOST   23.____
    NEARLY

    A. 15   B. 20   C. 25   D. 30

24. The percentage of the population over age 65 in the neighborhood described above is 24.____
    MOST NEARLY

    A. 2   B. 4   C. 6   D. 8

25.   25.____

    [Diagram: A large rectangle with a smaller rectangle inside labeled "TOWER". Below the diagram is a double-headed arrow labeled "800 ft" spanning the width of the large rectangle.]

    Assume that the above drawing has been made to scale. The total gross floor area of
    the 20-story tower is, in square feet, MOST NEARLY

       A. 200,000   B. 100,000   C. 1,000   D. 50,000

KEY (CORRECT ANSWERS)

1. A
2. D
3. D
4. D
5. D

6. B
7. B
8. A
9. A
10. C

11. C
12. B
13. A
14. A
15. C

16. C
17. D
18. B
19. D
20. A

21. C
22. C
23. B
24. D
25. A

TEST 2

DIRECTIONS: Each question or incomplete statement is followed by several suggested answers or completions. Select the one that BEST answers the question or completes the statement. *PRINT THE LETTER OF THE CORRECT ANSWER IN THE SPACE AT THE RIGHT.*

1. In the city, the body that is responsible for choosing the specific location of sites for public improvement is the

    A. city planning commission
    B. department of public works
    C. site selection board
    D. fine arts commission

2. Publicly-sponsored Early Childhood programs in the city do NOT include

    A. Family Day Care
    B. Headstart Program
    C. playschools for 2- and 3-year olds
    D. pre-kindergarten in elementary schools

3. The one of the following that is NOT a current method of controlling pollution is the

    A. requirement that incinerators in the city be upgraded
    B. project for recycling waste paper and aluminum goods for re-use
    C. sale of non-leaded gasoline for automobiles
    D. conversion of all combined sewers in the city to separate sanitary and storm sewers

4. In general, the MOST accurate 5-year projection of population can be made for the

    A. nation   B. metropolitan area
    C. inner city   D. neighborhood

5. The type of area in which the GREATEST percentage increase in population occurred between 1960 and 1980 was in the

    A. central cities   B. suburban rings
    C. rural non-farm areas D. rural farm areas

6. The one of the following that should NOT be included in a community planning study undertaken by a city planning department is

    A. a survey of how land is used in the area
    B. compilation of data on school utilization
    C. determination of rent levels in the area
    D. renovation of an old building at rents suitable for low-income people

7. The one of the following men who had a role in laying out cities along the formal lines of the *City Beautiful* movement was

    A. Rexford Tugwell   B. Daniel Burnham
    C. Clarence Stein   D. Frank Lloyd Wright

8. A key factor leading to the development of suburban growth in recent decades is

   A. a series of regional government compacts
   B. the large increase in automobile ownership
   C. the drying up of immigration
   D. the gradual shifting of some shopping and employment from the center of the city to the outskirts

9. A controlled aerial mosaic photograph would be LEAST useful in which of the following types of planning work?

   A. Land use study of undeveloped land
   B. Review of subdivision plats
   C. Study of proposed highway locations
   D. Building condition study of CBD

10. The MAJOR function of the city community planning boards is

    A. to prepare capital and expense budgets for community planning districts
    B. to advise the county executives and city agencies on planning issues
    C. as an umbrella organization for local poverty groups
    D. to provide technical planning help to local community groups

11. Special revenue sharing is intended to

    A. be available only for cities of over 1 million population
    B. be available for general purpose use, to be determined by the cities
    C. replace money previously distributed to cities for categorical grants
    D. in all instances be passed from the state to the city

12. The city's water pollution control plants are being upgraded to _____ treatment which removes _____.

    A. primary; "approximately" 65% of pollutants
    B. secondary; approximately 90% of pollutants
    C. tertiary; approximately 99% of pollutants
    D. desalination; all the mineral matter

13. *Turnkey* housing refers to

    A. a method of housing construction whereby a private developer finances and constructs the housing to the city's standards and the housing is then purchased by the city
    B. the conversion of old-law housing to co-op housing in moderate rent areas, including rent subsidies for low-income families
    C. brownstone renovation with no public subsidy in historic districts where the design must be approved by the landmarks commission
    D. a form of mixing housing with commercial or industrial space, as in the incentive zoning amendment

14. The Planned-Unit Development is a provision of the city zoning resolution which

   A. provides for industrial development on the outskirts of the city
   B. requires the building of schools, community centers, and shopping facilities as part of a large residential development
   C. permits housing to be built close together in clusters, leaving substantial land areas in their natural state as common open spaces
   D. provides a means of constructing off-street parking facilities in high density residential neighborhoods

15. The official map differs from the master plan in that it

   A. deals only with proposed streets as they relate to existing streets
   B. includes a detailed engineering design for the existing and proposed street system
   C. is an accurate description of the location of public improvements existing and proposed
   D. is tied directly to the Capital Budget and Improvement Program

16. According to the zoning resolution, a legal non-conforming use in zoning is one established

   A. prior to the adoption of the ordinance provision prohibiting it
   B. by a special exception permit issued by the planning commission
   C. by a variance issued by the board of standards and appeals
   D. for many years despite the prohibition in the ordinance and which had not been proceeded against

17. The formula for financing interstate highways under state and Federal law provides that the government of the city shall pay what percent of the cost of highway construction?

   A. 100%   B. 90%   C. 40%   D. 0%

18. The one of the following statements that MOST NEARLY expresses the city's long-term program in regard to arterial highways is to

   A. provide many routes throughout the city in order to minimize travel time from all points
   B. provide quick vehicular access from the business center to the suburbs
   C. build up bypass routes to discourage traffic from entering the business center
   D. build up the highway network in the outer boroughs and to landbank land in the business center for future through routes

19. The city planning commission

   A. consists of lifetime members, who annually elect a chairman
   B. administers the zoning resolution and hears appeals for variances
   C. prepares the annual 5-year capital improvement plan
   D. prepares the architectural designs for all public buildings, except schools

20. The feature of the city zoning resolution before 1961 which gave the city's skyscrapers their MOST distinctive architectural character was its 20._____

    A. height bonus for added setbacks
    B. rear yard provisions
    C. off-street parking and loading requirements
    D. density restrictions

KEY (CORRECT ANSWERS)

1.	C	11.	C
2.	C	12.	B
3.	D	13.	A
4.	A	14.	C
5.	B	15.	A
6.	D	16.	A
7.	B	17.	D
8.	B	18.	C
9.	D	19.	C
10.	B	20.	A

TEST 3

DIRECTIONS: Each question or incomplete statement is followed by several suggested answers or completions. Select the one that BEST answers the question or completes the statement. *PRINT THE LETTER OF THE CORRECT ANSWER IN THE SPACE AT THE RIGHT.*

Questions 1-3.

DIRECTIONS: Questions 1 through 3, inclusive, are to be answered in accordance with the following paragraphs.

Into the nine square miles that make up Manhattan's business districts, about two million people travel each weekday to go to work — the equivalent of the combined populations of Boston, Baltimore, and Cincinnati. Some 140,000 drive there in cars, 200,000 take buses, and 100,000 ride the commuter railroads. The great majority, however, go by subway — approximately 1.4 million people.

It is some ride. The last major improvement in the subway system was completed in 1935. The subways are dirty and noisy. Many local lines operate well beneath capacity; but many express lines are strained way beyond capacity in particular, the lines to Manhattan, now overloaded by 39,000 passengers during peak hours.

But for all its discomforts, the subway system is inherently a far more efficient way of moving people than automobiles and highways. Making this system faster, more convenient, and more comfortable for people must be the core of the city's transportation effort.

1. The CENTRAL point of the above text is that 1.____
   A. the equivalent of the combined populations of Boston, Baltimore, and Cincinnati commute into Manhattan's business district each weekday
   B. the improvement of the subway system is the key to the solution of moving people efficiently in and out of Manhattan's business district
   C. the subways are dirty and noisy, resulting in a terrible ride
   D. we should increase the ability of people to get in and out of Manhattan by cars, subways, and commuter railroads in order to ease the load from the subways

2. In accordance with the above paragraphs, 1.4 million people commute by subway and 2.____
   _____ by other mass transportation means.
   A. 200,000   B. 100,000   C. 440,000   D. 300,000

3. From the information given in the above paragraphs, one could logically conclude that, next to the subways, the transportation system that carries the LARGEST number of passengers is (the) 3.____
   A. railroads   B. cars
   C. buses   D. local lines

Questions 4-6.

DIRECTIONS: Questions 4 through 6, inclusive, are to be answered in accordance with the following paragraphs.

Incentive zoning is an affirmative tool that has widespread applications. The Zoning Resolution which became effective in 1981 substantially reduced the amount of floor space that a developer could put up on a given size lot and increased the light and air. In the Chrysler Building, which was built under the old legislation, the floor space is 27 times the size of the lot. The maximum ratio allowed for buildings now without a special permit is 18.

The newer zoning ordinance provided incentives to developers to devote part of the plot to public plazas or arcades. This space is needed to supplement the sidewalks, which in many cases are as narrow as they were when the midtown area was lined with brownstone or brickfront houses.

While the newer zoning has produced plazas, it has not of itself proved to be a sufficient development control. Stretches of Third Avenue and the Avenue of the Americas, for example, have been almost completely redeveloped in the last few years. This massive private investment has produced several fine individual buildings. The total environment produced, however, has been disappointing in a number of respects, and there is nowhere near the amenity that there could have been.

4. According to the paragraphs above, the use of incentive zoning has not been entirely successful because it has

   A. discouraged redevelopment
   B. encouraged massive private development along Third Avenue
   C. been ineffective in controlling overall redevelopment
   D. not significantly increased the number of parks and plazas being built

5. According to the above paragraphs, one might conclude that before the new Zoning Resolution was passed,

   A. buildings on a given site were required to have greater setbacks
   B. the amount of private investment in development was significantly smaller than it is today
   C. no controls on development existed
   D. the provision of parks and plazas was less frequent

6. In the context of the above paragraphs, the word *amenity* means

   A. compliance with regulations
   B. correction of undesirable environmental aspects
   C. responsiveness to guidelines and incentives
   D. pleasant or desirable features

Questions 7-8.

DIRECTIONS: Questions 7 and 8 are to be answered in accordance with the following paragraphs.

We must also find better ways to handle the relocation of people uprooted by projects. In the past, many renewal plans have foundered on this problem, and it is still the most difficult part of community development. Large-scale replacement of low-income residents — many ineligible for public housing — has contributed to deterioration of surrounding communities, as in Manhattan's West Side, Coney Island, and Arverne. Recently, thanks to changes in Housing Authority procedures, relocation has been accomplished in a far more satisfactory fashion. The step-by-step community development projects we advocate in this plan should bring further improvement.

But additional measures will be necessary. There are going to be more people to be moved; and, with the current shortage of apartments, large ones especially, it is going to be tougher to find places to move them to. The city should have more freedom to buy or lease housing that comes on the market because of normal turnover and make it available to relocatees.

7. According to the above paragraphs, one of the reasons a neighborhood may deteriorate is that

   A. there is a scarcity of large apartments
   B. step-by-step community development projects have failed
   C. people in the given neighborhood are uprooted from their homes
   D. a nearby renewal project has an inadequate relocation plan

7.____

8. From the above paragraphs, one might conclude that the relocation phase of community renewal has been improved

   A. by changes in Housing Authority procedures
   B. by development of step-by-step community development projects
   C. through expanded city powers to buy housing for relocation
   D. through the Housing Authority Leasing Program

8.____

Questions 9-10.

DIRECTIONS: Questions 9 and 10 are to be answered in accordance with the following paragraphs.

Provision of decent housing for the lower half of the population (by income) was thus taken on as a public responsibility. Public housing was to assist the poorest quarter of urban families while the 221(d)(3) Housing Program would assist the next quarter. But limited funds meant that the supply of subsidized housing could not stretch nearly far enough to help this half of the population. Who were to be left out in the rationing process which was accomplished by the sifting of applicants for housing on the part of public and private authorities?

Discrimination on the grounds of race or color is not allowed under Federal law. In all sections of the country, encouragingly, housing programs are found which allow this law to the letter. Yet, housing programs in some cities still suffer from the residue of racial segregation policies and attitudes that for years were condoned or even encouraged.

Some sifting in the 221(d)(3) Housing Program follows the practice of many public housing authorities, the imposition of requirements with respect to character. This is a delicate matter. To fill a project overwhelmingly with broken families, alcoholics, criminals, delinquents, and other problem tenants would hardly make it a wholesome environment. Yet the total exclusion of such families is hardly an acceptable alternative. To the extent this exclusion is practiced, the very people whose lives are described in order to persuade lawmakers and the public to instigate new programs find the door shut in their faces when such programs come into being. The proper balance is difficult to achieve, but society's neediest families surely should not be totally denied the opportunities for rejuvenation in subsidized housing.

9. From the above paragraphs, it can be assumed that the 221(d)(3) Housing Program 9.____

   A. served a population earning more than the median income
   B. served a less affluent population than is served by public housing
   C. excludes all problem families from its projects
   D. is a subsidized housing program

10. According to the above paragraphs, the provision of housing for the poor 10.____

    A. has not been completely accomplished with public monies
    B. is never influenced by segregationist policies
    C. is limited to providing housing for only the neediest families
    D. is primarily the responsibility of the Federal government

Questions 11-12.

DIRECTIONS: Questions 11 and 12 are to be answered in accordance with the following paragraph.

Though the recent trend toward apartment construction may appear to be the region's response to large-lot zoning and centralized industry, it really is not. It is mainly a function of the age of the population (coupled with a rush to build apartments in the city between the passage of the newer zoning ordinance and its enforcement in December 1981). Most of the apartments are occupied by one- and two-person families — young people out of school but without a family of their own and older people whose children have grown. Both groups have been increasing in number; and, in this region, they characteristically live in apartments. It is this increased demand for apartments and the simultaneous decrease in demand for one-family houses that dramatically raised the percentage of building permits issued for multi-family housing units from 36 percent in 1977 to 67 percent in 1981. The fact that three-fourths of the apartments were built in the Core between 1977 and 1981 at the same time as the Core was losing population underscores the failure of the apartment boom to slow the outward spread of the population.

11. According to the above paragraph, one of the reasons for the increase in the number of building permits issued for multi-family construction in the city metropolitan region is 11.____

    A. that workers in industry want to live close to their jobs
    B. an increase in the number of elderly people living in the region
    C. the inability of many families to afford the large lots necessary to build private homes
    D. the new zoning ordinance made it easier to build apartments

12. According to the above paragraph, the apartment construction boom 12.____

    A. increased the population density in the core
    B. spurred a population shift to the suburbs
    C. did not halt the outward flow of the population from the core
    D. was most significant in the outer areas of the region

Questions 13-14.

DIRECTIONS: Questions 13 and 14 are to be answered in accordance with the following paragraphs.

The city's economy has its own dynamics, and there is only so much the government can do to shape it. But that margin is critically important. If the city uses its points of leverage, it can generate a large number of jobs and good jobs, jobs that lead to advancement.

As a major employer itself, the city can upgrade the jobs it offers and greatly improve its services to the public if it does so. Since highly skilled professionals will always be in short supply, the city must train more paraprofessionals to take over routine tasks. Equally important, it must provide them with a realistic job ladder so they can move on up — nurse's aide to certified nurse, for example, teacher's aide to teacher. The training programs for such upgrading will require a substantial public investment but the cost-benefit return should be excellent.

As a major purchaser of goods and services, the city can stimulate business enterprise in the ghetto. The growth of Black and Puerto Rican firms will produce more local jobs; it will also create the kind of managerial talent the ghetto needs.

New kinds of enterprise can be set up. In housing, for example, there is a huge backlog of rehabilitation work to be done and a large pool of unskilled manpower to be trained for it. Corporations can be formed to take over tenements, remodel, maintain, and operate them, as in the Brownsville Home Maintenance Program. Grocery cooperatives to bring food prices down are another possibility.

13. According to the above paragraphs, the city is the major employer and, by using its capacity, it can

    A. assist unskilled people with talent to move up on the job ladder
    B. create private enterprises that will renew all areas of the city in need of renewal
    C. eliminate poverty in the ghetto areas by selective purchase of goods and services
    D. have no influence on the economy of the city

14. According to the above paragraphs, one may REASONABLY conclude that

    A. the city has no power to influence the job market
    B. a by-product of strategic purchasing and employment and training practices can be the rehabilitation of housing and the lowering of food prices
    C. highly skilled professions, which are now in short supply, will no longer be needed after paraprofessionals are trained to take over routine jobs
    D. the city's major objective is to bring down food prices

15. 500 persons attended a public hearing at which a proposed public housing project was being considered. Less than half favored the project, while the majority opposed the project.
    According to the above statement, it is REASONABLE to conclude that

    A. the proposal stimulated considerable community interest
    B. the public housing project was disapproved by the city because a majority opposed it

C. those who opposed the project lacked sympathy for needy persons
D. the supporters of the project were led by militants

16. A document was published by a public agency and distributed for discussion. The document contained data showing trends in the level of reading among freshmen college students and suggested that the high schools were not investing enough effort in overcoming retardation. It compared the costs of intensifying reading instruction in the secondary schools as compared to costs in college for such instruction.
According to the above statement, it is REASONABLE to conclude that

   A. the document proposed new programs
   B. the college students read better than high school students
   C. some college students need remedial reading
   D. the study was done by a consultant

17. A vacant lot close to a polluted creek is for sale. Two buyers compete. One owns an adjacent factory which provides 300 high paying unskilled jobs. He needs to expand or move from the city. If he expands, he will provide 300 additional jobs. The other is a community group in a changing residential area close by. They hope to stabilize the neighborhood by bringing in new housing. They could build an apartment building with 100 dwelling units on the lot.
According to the above paragraph, it is REASONABLE to conclude that

   A. jobs are more important than housing
   B. there is conflict between the factory owners and the neighborhood group
   C. the neighborhood group will not succeed in stabilizing the area by constructing new housing
   D. the polluted creek should be cleaned up

Questions 18-21.

DIRECTIONS: Questions 18 through 21, inclusive, refer to the phrases shown below. For each of the questions, select that phrase which BEST completes the sentence for that question.

   A. to increase training and educational opportunities
   B. to remove social ills by a slum clearance program
   C. to select the goals and values to which these resources should be directed
   D. to diminish drastic redevelopment, to provide opportunities to move within the area, or to move to new areas which can be assimilated to old objectives

18. In addition to concern with the rational allocation of resources, the urban planning process needs _____.

19. The early housing reformers emphasized the inadequate physical environment of the slums, understressed the connection between the social environment of the slums and the disorders they wanted to cure, and attempted _____.

20. The objective for assisting the transition to middle class status will mean intensified efforts _____. 20.____

21. To provide a sense of continuity for those people whose residential areas are being renewed, mainly working class, it is desirable _____. 21.____

Questions 22-25.

DIRECTIONS: For Questions 22 through 25, select that item from Column B that is MOST closely related to the item in Column A.

COLUMN A	COLUMN B	
22. City Map	A. Citizen Participation	22.____
23. Revenue Sharing	B. Block Grants	23.____
24. Opportunity Structure	C. Streets	24.____
25. Public Hearing	D. Upward Mobility	25.____

KEY (CORRECT ANSWERS)

1. B
2. D
3. C
4. C
5. D

6. D
7. D
8. A
9. D
10. A

11. B
12. C
13. A
14. B
15. A

16. C
17. B
18. C
19. B
20. A

21. D
22. C
23. B
24. D
25. A

EXAMINATION SECTION
TEST 1

DIRECTIONS: Each question or incomplete statement is followed by several suggested answers or completions. Select the one that BEST answers the question or completes the statement. *PRINT THE LETTER OF THE CORRECT ANSWER IN THE SPACE AT THE RIGHT.*

1. An interview is BEST conducted in private primarily because
   A. the person interviewed will tend to be less self-conscious
   B. the interviewer will be able to maintain his continuity of thought better
   C. it will insure that the interview is "off the record"
   D. people tend to "show off" before an audience

2. An interviewer can BEST establish a good relationship with the person being interviewed by
   A. assuming casual interest in the statements made by the person being interviewed
   B. taking the point of view of the person interviewed
   C. controlling the interview to a major extent
   D. showing a genuine interest in the person

3. An interviewer will be better able to understand the person interviewed and his problems if he recognizes that much of the person's behavior is due to motives
   A. which are deliberate
   B. of which he is unaware
   C. which are inexplicable
   D. which are kept under control

4. An interviewer's attention must be directed toward himself as well as toward the person interviewed.
   This statement means that the interviewer should
   A. keep in mind the extent to which his own prejudices may influence his judgment
   B. rationalize the statements made by the person interviewed
   C. gain the respect and confidence of the person interviewed
   D. avoid being too impersonal

5. More complete expression will be obtained from a person being interviewed if the interviewer can create the impression that
   A. the data secured will become part of a permanent record
   B. official information must be accurate in every detail
   C. it is the duty of the person interviewed to give accurate data
   D. the person interviewed is participating in a discussion of his own problems

6. The practice of asking leading questions should be avoided in an interview   6.____
   because the
   A. interviewer risks revealing his attitudes to the person being interviewed
   B. interviewer may be led to ignore the objective attitudes of the person
      interviewed
   C. answers may be unwarrantedly influenced
   D. person interviewed will resent the attempt to lead him and will be less
      cooperative

7. A good technique for the interviewer to use in an effort to secure reliable data   7.____
   and to reduce the possibility of misunderstanding is to
   A. use casual undirected conversation, enabling the person being
      interviewed to talk about himself, and thus secure the desired information
   B. adopt the procedure of using direct questions regularly
   C. extract the desired information from the person being interviewed by
      putting him on the defensive
   D. explain to the person being interviewed the information desired and the
      reason for needing it

8. You are interviewing a patient to determine whether she is eligible for medical   8.____
   assistance. Of the many questions that you have to ask her, some are routine
   questions that patients tend to answer willingly and easily. Other questions are
   more personal and some patients tend to resent being asked them and avoid
   answering them directly.
   For you to begin the interview with the more personal questions would be
   A. *desirable*, because the end of the interview will go smoothly and the
      patient will be left with a warm feeling
   B. *undesirable*, because the patient might not know the answers to the
      questions
   C. *desirable*, because you will be able to return to these questions later to
      verify the accuracy of the responses
   D. *undesirable*, because you might antagonize the patient before you have
      had a chance to establish rapport

9. While interviewing a patient about her family composition, the patient asks you   9.____
   whether you are married.
   Of the following, the MOST appropriate way for you to handle this situation is to
   A. answer the question briefly and redirect her back to the topic under
      discussion
   B. refrain from answering the question and proceed with the interview
   C. advise the patient that it is more important that she answer your questions
      than that you answer hers, and proceed with the interview
   D. promise the patient that you will answer her question later, in the hope
      that she will forget, and redirect her back to the topic under discussion

10. In response to a question about his employment history, a patient you are   10.____
    interviewing rambles and talks about unrelated matters.
    Of the following, the MOST appropriate course of action for you to take FIRST
    is to

A. ask questions to direct the patient back to his employment history
B. advise him to concentrate on your questions and not to discuss irrelevant information
C. ask him why he is resisting a discussion of his employment history
D. advise him that if you cannot get the information you need, he will not be eligible for medical assistance

11. Suppose that a person you are interviewing becomes angry at some of the questions you have asked, calls you meddlesome and nosy, and states that she will not answer those questions.
    Of the following, which is the BEST action for you to take?
    A. Explain the reasons the questions are asked and the importance of the answers
    B. Inform the interviewee that you are only doing your job and advise her that she should answer your questions or leave the office
    C. Report to your supervisor what the interviewee called you and refuse to continue the interview
    D. End the interview and tell the interviewee she will not be serviced by your department

12. Suppose that during the course of an interview the interviewee demands in a very rude way that she be permitted to talk to your supervisor or someone in charge.
    Which of the following is probably the BEST way to handle this situation?
    A. Inform your supervisor of the demand and ask her to speak to the interviewee
    B. Pay no attention to the demands of the interviewee and continue the interview
    C. Report to your supervisor and tell her to get another interviewer for this interviewee
    D. Tell her you are the one "in charge" and that she should talk to you

13. Of the following, the outcome of an interview by an aide depends MOST heavily on the
    A. personality of the interviewee
    B. personality of the aide
    C. subject matter of the questions asked
    D. interaction between aide and interviewee

14. Some patients being interviewed are primarily interested in making a favorable impression.
    The aide should be aware of the fact that such patients are more likely than other patients to
    A. try to anticipate the answers the interviewer is looking for
    B. answer all questions openly and frankly
    C. try to assume the role of interviewer
    D. be anxious to get the interview over as quickly as possible

15. The type of interview which an aide usually conducts is substantially different from most interviewing situations in all of the following aspects EXCEPT the
    A. setting
    B. kinds of clients
    C. techniques employed
    D. kinds of problems

16. During an interview, an aide uses a "leading question."
    This type of question is so-called because it generally
    A. starts a series of questions about one topic
    B. suggests the answer which the aide wants
    C. forms the basis for a following "trick" question
    D. sets, at the beginning, the tone of the interview

17. Casework interviewing is always directed to the client and his situation.
    The one of the following which is the MOST accurate statement with respect to the proper focus of an interview is that the
    A. caseworker limits the client to concentration on objective data
    B. client is generally permitted to talk about facts and feelings with no direction from the caseworker
    C. main focus in casework interviews is on feelings rather than facts
    D. caseworker is responsible for helping the client focus on any material which seems to be related to his problems or difficulties

18. Assume that you are conducting a training program for the caseworkers under your supervision. At one of the sessions, you discuss the problem of interviewing a dull and stupid client who gives a slow and disconnected case history.
    The BEST of the following interviewing methods for you to recommend in such a case in order to ascertain facts is for the caseworker to
    A. ask the client leading questions requiring "yes" or "no" answers
    B. request the client to limit his narration to the essential facts so that the interview can be kept as brief as possible
    C. review the story with the client, patiently asking simple questions
    D. tell the client that unless he is more cooperative he cannot be helped to solve his problem

19. A recent development in casework interviewing procedure, known as multiple-client interviewing, consists of interviews of the entire family at the same time. However, this may not be an effective casework method in certain situations. Of the following, the situation in which the standard individual interview would be preferable is when
    A. family member derive consistent and major gratification from assisting each other in their destructive responses
    B. there is a crucial family conflict to which the members are reacting
    C. the family is overwhelmed by interpersonal anxieties which have not been explored
    D. the worker wants to determine the pattern of family interaction to further his diagnostic understanding

20. A follow-up interview was arranged for an applicant in order that he could furnish 20.____
certain requested evidence. At this follow-up interview, the applicant still fails
to furnish the necessary evidence.
It would be MOST advisable for you to
   A. advise the applicant that he is now considered ineligible
   B. ask the applicant how soon he can get the necessary evidence and set a
      date for another interview
   C. question the applicant carefully and thoroughly to determine if he has
      misrepresented or falsified any information
   D. set a date for another interview and tell the applicant to get the necessary
      evidence by that time

KEY (CORRECT ANSWERS)

1.	A	11.	A
2.	D	12.	A
3.	B	13.	D
4.	A	14.	A
5.	D	15.	C
6.	C	16.	B
7.	D	17.	D
8.	D	18.	C
9.	A	19.	A
10.	A	20.	B

TEST 2

DIRECTIONS: Each question or incomplete statement is followed by several suggested answers or completions. Select the one that BEST answers the question or completes the statement. *PRINT THE LETTER OF THE CORRECT ANSWER IN THE SPACE AT THE RIGHT.*

1. In interviewing, the practice of anticipating an applicant's answers to questions is generally
    A. *desirable*, because it is effective and economical when it is necessary to interview large numbers of applicants
    B. *desirable*, because many applicants have language difficulties
    C. *undesirable*, because it is the inalienable right of every person to answer as he sees fit
    D. *undesirable*, because applicants may tend to agree with the answer proposed by the interviewer even when the answer is not entirely correct

2. When an initial interview is being conducted, one way of starting is to explain the purpose of the interview to the applicant.
    The practice of starting the interview with such an explanation is generally
    A. *desirable*, because the applicant can then understand why the interview is necessary and what will be accomplished by it
    B. *desirable*, because it creates the rapport which is necessary to successful interviewing
    C. *undesirable*, because time will be saved by starting directly with the questions which must be asked
    D. *undesirable*, because the interviewer should have the choice of starting an interview in any manner he prefers

3. For you to use responses such as "That's interesting," "Uh-huh," and "Good" during an interview with a patient is
    A. *desirable*, because they indicate that the investigator is attentive
    B. *undesirable*, because they are meaningless to the patient
    C. *desirable*, because the investigator is not supposed to talk excessively
    D. *undesirable*, because they tend to encourage the patient to speak freely

4. During the course of a routine interview, the BEST tone of voice for an interviewer to use is
    A. authoritative   B. uncertain
    C. formal   D. conversational

5. It is recommended that interviews which inquire into the personal background of an individual should be held in private.
    The BEST reason for this practice is that privacy
    A. allows the individual to talk freely about the details of his background
    B. induces contemplative thought on the part of the interviewed individual
    C. prevents any interruptions by departmental personnel during the interview
    D. most closely resembles the atmosphere of the individual's personal life

6. Assume that you are interviewing a patient to determine whether he has any savings accounts.
   To obtain this information, the MOST effective way to phrase your question would be:
   A. "You don't have any savings, do you?"
   B. "At which bank do you have a savings account?"
   C. "Do you have a savings account?"
   D. "May I assume that you have a savings account?"

7. You are interviewing a patient who is not cooperating to the extent necessary to get all required information. Therefore, you decide to be more forceful in your approach.
   In this situation, such a course of action is
   A. *advisable*, because such a change in approach may help to increase the patient's participation
   B. *advisable*, because you will be using your authority more effectively
   C. *inadvisable*, because you will not be able to change this approach if it doesn't produce results
   D. *inadvisable*, because an aggressive approach generally reduces the validity of the interview

8. You have attempted to interview a patient on two separate occasions, and both attempts were unsuccessful. The patient has been totally uncooperative and you sense a personal hostility toward you.
   Of the following, the BEST way to handle this type of situation would be to
   A. speak to the patient in a courteous manner and ask him to explain exactly what he dislikes about you
   B. inform the patient that you will not allow personality conflicts to disrupt the interview
   C. make no further attempt to interview the patient and recommend that he be billed in full
   D. discuss the problem with your supervisor and suggest that another investigator be assigned to try to interview the patient

9. At the beginning of an interview, a patient with normal vision tells you that he is reluctant to discuss his finances. You realize that it will be necessary in this case to ask detailed questions about his net income.
   When you begin this line of questioning, of the following, the LEAST important aspect you should consider is your
   A. precise wording of the question   B. manner of questioning
   C. tone of voice   D. facial expressions

10. A caseworker under your supervision has been assigned the task of interviewing a man who is applying for foster home placement for his two children. The caseworker seeks your advice as to how to question this man, stating that she finds the applicant to be a timid and self-conscious person who seems torn between the necessity of having to answer the worker's questions truthfully and the effect he thinks his answers will have on his application.

Of the following, the BEST method for the caseworker to use in order to determine the essential facts in this case is to
- A. assure the applicant that he need not worry since the majority of applications for foster home placement are approved
- B. delay the applicant's narration of the facts important to the case until his embarrassment and fears have been overcome
- C. ignore the statements made by the applicant and obtain all the required information from his friends and relatives
- D. inform the applicant that all statements made by him will be verified and are subject to the law governing perjury

11. Assume that a worker is interviewing a boy in his assigned group in order to help him find a job.
At the BEGINNING of the interview, the worker should
    - A. suggest a possible job for the youth
    - B. refer the youth to an employment agency
    - C. discuss the youth's work history and skills with him
    - D. refer the youth to the manpower and career development agency

11._____

12. As part of the investigation to locate an absent father, you make a field visit to interview one of the father's friends. Before beginning the interview, you identify yourself to the friend and show him your official identification.
For you to do this is, generally,
    - A. *good practice*, because the friend will have proof that you are authorized to make such confidential investigations
    - B. *poor practice*, because the friend may not answer your questions when he knows why you are interviewing him
    - C. *good practice*, because your supervisor can confirm from the friend that you actually made the interview
    - D. *poor practice*, because the friend may warn the absent father that your agency is looking for him

12._____

13. You are interviewing a client in his home as part of your investigation of an anonymous complaint that he has been receiving Medicaid fraudulently. During the interview, the client frequently interrupts your questions to discuss the hardships of his life and the bitterness he feels about his medical condition.
Of the following, the BEST way for you to deal with these discussions is to
    - A. cut them off abruptly, since the client is probably just trying to avoid answering your questions
    - B. listen patiently, since these discussions may be helpful to the client and may give you information for your investigation
    - C. remind the client that you are investigating a complaint against him and he must answer directly
    - D. seek to gain the client's confidence by discussing any personal or medical problems which you yourself may have

13._____

14. While interviewing an absent father to determine his ability to pay child support, you realize that his answers to some of your questions contradict his answers to other questions.
Of the following, the BEST way for you to try to get accurate information from the father is to
   A. confront him with his contradictory answers and demand an explanation from him
   B. use your best judgment as to which of his answers are accurate and question him accordingly
   C. tell him that he has misunderstood your questions and that he must clarify his answers
   D. ask him the same questions in different words and follow up his answer with related questions

15. Assume that an applicant, obviously under a great deal of stress, talks continuously and rambles, making it difficult for you to determine the exact problem and her need.
In order to make the interview more successful, it would be BEST for you to
   A. interrupt the applicant and ask her specific questions in order to get the information you need
   B. tell the applicant that her rambling may be a basic cause of her problem
   C. let the applicant continue talking as long as she wishes
   D. ask the applicant to get to the point because other people are waiting for you

16. A worker must be able to interview clients all day and still be able to listen and maintain interest.
Of the following, it is MOST important for you to show interest in the client because, if you appear interested,
   A. the client is more likely to appreciate your professional status
   B. the client is more likely to disclose a greater amount of information
   C. the client is less likely to tell lie
   D. you are more likely to gain your supervisor's approval

17. When you are interviewing clients, it is important to notice and record how they say what they say—angrily, nervously, or with "body English"—because these signs may
   A. tell you that the client's words are the opposite of what the client feels and you may need to dig to find out what those feeling are
   B. be the prelude to violent behavior which no aide is prepared to handle
   C. show that the client does not really deserve serious consideration
   D. be important later should you be asked to defend what you did for the client

18. The patient you are interviewing is reticent and guarded in responding to your questions. He is not providing the information needed to complete his application for medical assistance.
In this situation, the one of the following which is the MOST appropriate course of action for you to take FIRST is to

A. end the interview and ask him to contact you when he is ready to answer your questions
B. advise the patient that you cannot end the interview until he has provided all the information you need to complete the application
C. emphasize to the patient the importance of the questions and the need to answer them in order to complete the application
D. advise the patient that if he answers your questions the interview will be easier for both of you

19. At the end of an interview with a patient, he describes a problem he is having with his teenage son, who is often truant and may be using narcotics. The patient asks you for advice in handling his son.
Of the following, the MOST appropriate action for you to take is to
    A. make an appointment to see the patient and his son together
    B. give the patient a list of drug counseling programs to which he may refer his son
    C. suggest to the patient that his immediate concern should be his own hospitalization rather than his son's problem
    D. tell the patient that you are not qualified to assist him but will attempt to find out who can

20. A MOST appropriate condition in the use of direct questions to obtain personal data in an interview is that, whenever possible,
    A. the direct questions be used only as a means of encouraging the person interviewed to talk about himself
    B. provision be made for recording the information
    C. the direct questions be used only after all other methods have failed
    D. the person being interviewed understands the reason for requesting the information

KEY (CORRECT ANSWERS)

1.	D	11.	C
2.	A	12.	A
3.	A	13.	B
4.	D	14.	D
5.	A	15.	A
6.	B	16.	B
7.	A	17.	A
8.	D	18.	C
9.	A	19.	D
10.	B	20.	D

EXAMINATION SECTION
TEST 1

DIRECTIONS: Each of Questions 1 through 15 consists of a passage which contains one word that is incorrectly used because it is not in keeping with the meaning that the passage is evidently intended to convey. Determine which word is incorrectly used. Then select from the words lettered A, B, C, or D the word which, when substituted for the incorrectly used word, would BEST help to convey the meaning of the passage.

1. A manager must often operate systems that are quite complex, but these systems are an effective vehicle for management. Each system has an input, a process, and an output, and is a self-contained unit, but it is also related to a system of a wider and higher order as well as to its own sub-systems that represent the integration of several systems of the lower order. Thinking in terms of systems restricts his understanding of the multitudinous activities with which he must work, and it also enables him to see better the nature of the complex problems that he faces.

    A. isolation
    B. simplifies
    C. perpetuating
    D. constrains

2. Planning involves, first, the conceiving of goals and the development of alternative courses of future action to achieve the goals. Second, it involves the reduction of these alternatives from a very large number to a small number and finally to one approved course of action, the program. Budgeting probably plays a slight part in the first phase but an increasingly important and decisive part in the second. It facilitates the choice-making process by providing a basis for systematic comparisons among alternatives which take into account their total impacts on both the debit and the credit sides. It thus encourages, and provides some of the tools for, an increasing degree of precision in the planning process. Budgeting is the ingredient of planning which precedes the entire process.

    A. achievement
    B. improved
    C. immediate
    D. disciplines

3. In every instance the burden of proving each of the charges against the employee, which constitute the claimed misconduct or incompetence, must be upon the agency alleging the same. This simply means that it is incumbent upon the agency to establish each of the charges by a fair preponderance of the entire evidence. Unless the Hearing Officer is satisfied that the evidence has fairly and reasonably established the facts asserted by the agency, the agency has not sustained the burden of proof. The Hearing Officer must determine the admissibility of evidence where there is an objection to a question. Although at disciplinary hearings the presentation of the testimony is not limited by strict and technical rules of evidence as in a court, nevertheless the Hearing Officer should at all times consider its relevance and materiality, and then make his determination on the basis of fairness.

    A. corroborate
    B. incredible
    C. disinterested
    D. obligatory

4. The examination of alternative means available for the accomplishment of a given program must proceed along lines somewhat different from the review of alternative programs. In the former, the budget officer should possess sufficient knowledge of operations, and of methods and procedures, to be able to challenge badly conceived projects and to ask the kinds of questions which call forth the orderly processes of administration. This is where budget review and organization and method analysis tend to conflict, and it is here that the reviewing officer who has had operating experience can be most effective in questioning and criticizing management techniques.

   A. personnel
   B. problems
   C. public
   D. merge

5. The employee is not required to submit a written answer to the charges of incompetency or misconduct. The fact that an employee does not choose to submit a written answer should not be taken to mean that he admits guilt. However, the answer provides a means for the accused employee, in writing and for the record, to plead guilty or not guilty to the various charges and specifications, to allege matters tending to disprove the charges, including his good character and reputation, to allege any incriminating circumstances and also to plead a favorable record of service and conduct which might tend to lessen the penalty. Upon receipt of the employee's written answer to the charges, the answer should be carefully analyzed and any allegations therein verified. It may also be necessary to gather new evidence for the hearing in relation to allegations contained in the answer.

   A. confidential
   B. mitigative
   C. particularize
   D. procedural

6. In an article in the Harvard Business Review ("Human Relations or Human Resources"), Raymond E. Miles expounded a human resources theory of management. He declared that a manager's job cannot be viewed as merely one of giving direction and obtaining cooperation; rather, it is one of creating an environment in which the total resources of his department can be utilized. In this environment, the manager shares information and modifies departmental decisions with his employees and encourages their self-direction, not to improve their role satisfactions but to improve the decision making and the total performance efficiency of the organization. Many decisions are made more efficiently by those directly involved in and affected by them. In fact, Miles added, the more important the decisions, the greater the manager's obligation to encourage subordinate self-direction.

   A. actuate
   B. appearance
   C. compulsion
   D. discusses

7. Each organization follows a particular philosophy of management selected from a spectrum ranging from authoritarian to participative. If it adopts an approach in which the manager makes all the decisions and passes them on to subordinates for consideration, it follows an authoritarian philosophy that determines its organization structure and climate. Its structure will follow closely the pattern of many levels of management, tight spans of control, and formal channels of communication. The direction of information flow will be downward, supervisors will have little trust in subordinates, and a high degree of emphasis will be placed on management controls.

   A. approve
   B. concentrated
   C. discretionary
   D. execution

8. Besides the ability to comprehend the magnitude of decisions the ability to deal with decision complexity also differs from person to person. Most human beings are discouraged only with a two-option decision, seeing reality in terms of black or white and hardly ever noticing the gray. Even when there is a choice of three or four pretty well-defined options, a human being will consciously or unconsciously reduce them to two. It takes a good deal of training and education plus a highly developed intellectual structure to handle multi-option decisions and to actively seek a third or fourth alternative.

    A. comfortable   B. enlarging
    C. narrowly   D. passive

8.____

9. Manpower planning, like finance; is a management function that cannot be delegated or decentralized. What has often been overlooked in studies of decentralization is that no successful firm has ever decentralized the financial function. Since there has rarely been more than one treasurer in a firm, the centralized, control of finances exercises an auxiliary power over all members in a decentralized organization. Just as the management of financial resources is regularly centralized, so the management of human and, in particular, managerial resources must be centralized and the primary responsibility accepted by the chief executive. In fact, he should consider the direction of the managerial manpower plan to be his top responsibility.

    A. concentration   B. external
    C. subsidiary   D. ultimate

9.____

10. One drawback of the participative-management approach is the lack of solid research to document its contentions. What has been collected is either inconclusive or negative. Laboratory experiments have repeatedly demonstrated that groups that are organized to counter interpersonal comfort, openness, familiarity, and cohesiveness perform poorly. At least one study, in a large insurance company, of different styles of management revealed that while greater acceptance of leadership and high morale were present in the division led by the manager who believes in democratic supervision, this division's performance results were no better than those achieved by the authoritarian leaders.

    A. disputed   B. emphasise
    C. inconsistency   D. resistance

10.____

11. An organization experiences continuous changes which, taken together, tend to follow a course that can be defined and projected as a trend. Thus, after a company has accumulated sufficient historical data, it is fairly simple to project certain manpower trends. For example, to estimate within a fairly close margin the number of managers who will retire, die, resign, or be discharged in the succeeding 12 months is not so difficult. What is much more difficult and should not even be tried is to predict the number of those individuals who will die, retire, or resign. Simply knowing that, according to present trends, the company must replace 23 managers in the next 12 months is a distinct advantage, and knowing within certain confidence limits how many must be replaced within the next five years affords an even greater advantage

    A. handicap   B. names
    C. terminated   D. withheld

11.____

12. To assess another person, one must first obtain an accurate description of him in relation to the task for which he is being considered, But, to describe a person accurately, we must obtain relevant information about him and this is the sensitive area. Precisely what information is relevant to the role he is asked to play? If it is relevant, have we the right to it? Are there not some personal areas that are open for public inspection? These quite difficult questions are made even more difficult by the unfortunate way they have been raised recently by government agencies. The mishandling of inquiries into the personal background of applicants for positions has been so widespread that it has been necessary to pass laws at all levels restricting the amount and the quality of information that an employer may seek to obtain from a job applicant.

   A. disclosure
   B. processing
   C. prohibition
   D. unavailable

13. An organization's goals must be based on an accurate appraisal of its manpower resources, otherwise they will be like the objectives announced by a last-place baseball-team manager in the spring no more than pious hopes set down for their inspirational value. Public officials are quite guilty in this respects establishing targets for full employment, tax reduction, and urban renewal that are totally attainable and hardly within the capacities of those on the payroll. Many businesses follow the same practice, establishing market-penetration or sales goals that are quite beyond the competence and the energy of their employees. Setting goals, therefore, must take into account the probable course of events that is likely to unfold inside and outside the organization. This prediction of future events is known as forecasting.

   A. estimates
   B. laxity
   C. tendency
   D. unrealistic

14. In some organizations, a silent conspiracy can prevail that masks the facts about the managerial situation. Older managers who feel threatened by their advancing age, their creeping obsolescence, or their rapidly changing environment may try to hide their heads in the sands of yesterday. To support themselves, they may try many maneuvers — hiding promising young men, promoting incompetence, or making a farce out of the performance evaluation program. Out of this mass anxiety an "establishment" is born, a highly structured "in" group that invalidates manpower rules designed to insure its own security. This is the system that old men cherish and young men rail a gainst, that blights an organization like a creeping cancer and slowly destroys it as, all the while, its presence remains unfelt until it is fatal.

   A. enforces
   B. erosion
   C. manipulate
   D. terminating

15. Z. Pietrowski found that the successful top executive strives more intensively for personal achievement, sets more difficult work goals for himself, can adapt emotionally to a variety of people, is more original, and has less insecurity and self-doubt. E. Ghiselli found in his study of 287 managers that the effective manager showed less need for job security than did less effective managers. The effective managers showed the strongest desire for self-actualization, for the opportunity to utilize their talents in customary ways. In summary, the studies indicate quite clearly that the successful manager has a total life pattern of successful endeavor.

   A. conspicuously
   B. creative
   C. effacement
   D. ineffectual

KEY (CORRECT ANSWERS)

1. B
2. D
3. A
4. D
5. B

6. D
7. D
8. A
9. D
10. B

11. B
12. D
13. D
14. A
15. B

TEST 2

DIRECTIONS: Each of the following questions consists of a paragraph which contains one word that is incorrectly used because it is not in keeping with the meaning that the paragraph is evidently intended to convey. Determine which word is incorrectly used. Select from the choices lettered A, B, C, and D the word which, when substituted for the incorrectly used work, would BEST help to convey the meaning of the paragraph.

1. Among the Housing Manager's over-all responsibilities in administering a project is the prevention of the development of conditions which might lead to termination of tenancy and eviction of a tenant. Where there appears to be doubt that a tenant is fully aware of his responsibilities and is thus jeopardizing his tenancy, the Housing Manager should acquaint him with these responsibilities. Where a situation involves behavior of a tenant or a member of his family, the Housing Manager should confirm, through discussions and referrals to social agencies, correction of the conditions before they reach a stage where there is no alternative but termination proceedings.

   A. coordinate B. identify
   C. assert   D. attempt

1.____

2. There is one almost universal administrative complaint. The budget is inadequate, Now, between adequacy and inadequacy lie all degrees of adequacy. Further, human wants are modest in relation to human resources. From these two facts we may conclude that the fundamental criterion of administrative decision must be a criterion Of efficiency (the degree to which the goals have been reached relative to the available resources) rather than a criterion of adequacy (the degree to which its goals have been reached). The task of the administrator is to maximize social values relative to limited resources.

   A. improve   B. simple
   C. limitless D. optimize

2.____

3. Leadership is a personality characteristic based to a large extent on the charisma the leader possesses for his followers. Thus his appeal must be to the emotional and the personal life of the group. A manager, on the other hand, has been entrusted with the responsibility of decision making, which has nothing whatsoever to do with leadership. It is not a personal trait, it is a role that is not administrative and based upon the process of choosing a course of action and committing the group's resources to it. The manager's function is to define goals and objectives, to select a course of action to achieve them, and to evaluate realistically the results of that action. There is little charisma in such a role. Leaders depend for their success on personality, a characteristic that has nothing to do with management. Consequently, leadership and management are most appropriately treated as separate phenomena that are effectively handled simultaneously but not necessarily by the same person.

   A. initiates B. limit
   C. purely   D. rational

3.____

4. Where it appears that any City employee may be guilty of corruption or wrongdoing, the Department of Investigation should be informed. The agency itself should then conduct the inquiry immediately only if the Department of Investigation so determines. If during an inquiry it appears that the corruption or wrongdoing may be more serious or widespread than originally suspected, the Department of Investigation should be recontacted immediately. In some instances, it may be necessary to hold the disciplinary hearing prior to the criminal proceedings and it is essential that the conduct of the criminal case not be unnecessarily warranted by the department trial. The transcript and all papers should be kept in a secure place and there should be no disclosure or publicity about what transpired without the approval of the Corpora- tion Counsel and the Commissioner of Investigation.

   A. superseded   B. prejudiced
   C. premature   D. concurrently

5. It is often easy to enumerate reasons why a housing enterprise succeeds or fails. With so many variables that appear to have a make-or-break impact upon the outcome, there is a natural tendency to over-emphasize the importance of the man, particularly the man in charge. Society subscribes to the idea that housing leadership is important, but society doesn't really believe it. Even top housing managers are dubious about the significance of their own roles in the success or failure of a public enterprise. When things go wrong, they tend to blame the system; when things go right, they modestly give credit to "the team." The only way to manage a housing organization effectively is to give managers authority to run it and then hold them strictly accountable for the results. This idea is hardly new to anyone, however rarely it is carried out in practice. But the idea breaks down because we know so little about picking men who have the capacity to manage large housing enterprises.

   A. coalesce   B. disavows
   C. overlook   D. wavering

6. The technological and social changes that have occurred in American economy during the rise of the Managerial Society have not only required much more highly trained managers, they have created intense competition for these same men from other sectors of the economy: from the government, from education, and from the nonprofit areas. In the decade between 1954 and 1964, the number of employees in the executive classes of the federal government jumped 58 percent. The result is an unprecedented demand for managers that is likely to continue unabated for the next three decades. If we assume that the shortage has been met in the same way as in technical fields, it is probable that a substantial number of managerial positions are filled by people not fully qualified or that the positions have been reinforced by the inclusion of duties incompatible with those of a manager. Since this latter strategy is most commonly employed, it is possible to assert that many managers are managers in name only.

   A. conflicting   B. diluted
   C. eliminate   D. incumbent

7. There is also a suspicion in some quarters that admin- istrators have a tendency to be imperialistic, that government officials have an inborn desire to spend more of the tax-payers' money, to hire more people, to build more buildings. Sometimes this charge is couched in more gentle terms, it is suggested that administrators tend to overestimate simply to be on the safe side, so that they will be able to retain some leeway in program administration. Again, there is no doubt that these charges and suspicions are justified in particular cases. The overzealous and overambitious are not unknown in our society, or in any society. But it would be difficult to demonstrate that these tendencies are more widespread in government than elsewhere. Very often, what looks like an overweening ambition may turn out to be regressive administration. The government official who seeks to expand his program may do so because he sees the need, because he would like to do *a* better job, because he is close to the beneficiaries of his program operations.

    A. responsive
    B. fewer
    C. freedom
    D. targets

7.____

KEY (CORRECT ANSWERS)

1. D
2. C
3. C
4. B
5. C
6. B
7. A

EXAMINATION SECTION
TEST 1

DIRECTIONS: Each question or incomplete statement is followed by several suggested answers or completions. Select the one that BEST answers the question or completes the statement. *PRINT THE LETTER OF THE CORRECT ANSWER IN THE SPACE AT THE RIGHT.*

1. Suppose that one of the forms you fill out daily requires some information which you know is unnecessary.
   Which is the BEST action to take?
   A. Refuse to supply the information you think is unnecessary.
   B. Continue to fill out the form as required, even though the information is unnecessary.
   C. Suggest to your supervisor that the form be revised to reflect useful information.
   D. Suggest that fewer copies of the form be required.

   1.____

2. Of the following, the MOST likely reason for recommending that your department establish a standard form for recording certain information would be that this information
   A. will be produced at some disciplinary hearing
   B. concerns a secret or confidential record about an unusual incident at the garage
   C. contains a detailed explanation of a complex procedure
   D. must be taken from a large number of people on a regular basis

   2.____

3. If the four steps listed below for processing records were given in logical sequence, the one that would be the THIRD step is
   A. coding the records, using a chart or classification system
   B. inspecting the records to make sure they have been released for filing
   C. preparing cross-reference sheets or cards
   D. skimming the records to determine filing captions

   3.____

4. Which of the following BEST describes "office work simplification"?
   A. An attempt to increase the rate of production by speeding up the movements of employees
   B. Eliminating wasteful steps in order to increase efficiency
   C. Making jobs as easy as possible for employees so they will not be overworked
   D. Eliminating all difficult tasks from an office and leaving only simple ones

   4.____

5. The use of the same method of recordkeeping and reporting by all sections is
   A. *desirable*, mainly because it saves time in section operations
   B. *undesirable*, mainly because it kills the initiative of the individual section foreman
   C. *desirable*, mainly because it will be easier for the superior to evaluate and compare section operations
   D. *undesirable*, mainly because operations vary from section to section and uniform recordkeeping and reporting is not appropriate

5._____

6. The GREATEST benefit the section officer will have from keeping complete and accurate records of section operations is that
   A. he will find it easier to run his section efficiently
   B. he will need less equipment
   C. he will need less manpower
   D. the section will run smoothly when he is out

6._____

7. You have prepared a report to your superior and are ready to send it forward. But on reading it, you think some parts are not clearly expressed and the superior may have difficulty getting your point.
Of the following, it would be BEST for you to
   A. give the report to one of your men to read, and, if he has no trouble understanding it, send it through
   B. forward the report and call the superior the next day to ask if it was all right
   C. forward the report as is; higher echelons should be able to understand any report prepared by a section officer
   D. do the report over, re-writing the sections you are doubtful of

7._____

8. Of the following, a flow chart is BEST described as a chart which shows
   A. the places through which work moves in the course of the job process
   B. which employees perform specific functions leading to the completion of a job
   C. the schedules for production and how they eliminate waiting time between jobs
   D. how work units are affected by the actions of related work units

8._____

9. A superior decided to hold a problem-solving conference with his entire staff and distributed an announcement and agenda one week before the meeting.
Of the following, the BEST reason for providing each participate with an agenda is that
   A. participants will feel that something will be accomplished
   B. participants may prepare for the conference
   C. controversy will be reduced
   D. the top man should state the expected conclusions

9._____

10. The one of the following activities which is generally the LEAST proper function of a centralized procedures section is
    A. issuing new and revised procedural instructions
    B. coordinating forms revision and procedural changes
    C. accepting or rejecting authorized procedural changes
    D. controlling standard numbering systems for procedural releases

10.____

11. Assume that it is the policy of an operating unit to act on all requests received within five working days. Several operations are involved in acting on these requests. Each operation is performed by a separate sub-unit. The staff of the unit is reasonable adequate to handle this workload.
    If only one of the following can be done, the MOST effective procedure for maintaining adherence to the unit's five-day processing policy is to
    A. maintain a central "tickler" file in each sub-unit for the requests received daily in that sub-unit
    B. prepare a "tickler" card for each request and follow it up five days later to determine whether action has been taken
    C. rely on standards of production for each operation as an incentive to the employees of each sub-unit to meet the schedule
    D. schedule the operations on a timetable basis so that the request will be forwarded from one sub-unit to another within specified time limits

11.____

12. When one or two simple changes are needed in a memo to another unit or in a letter to a citizen, a unit head follows the practice of making such simple changes neatly in ink.
    This practice is GENERALLY
    A. *poor*, chiefly because it reflects unfavorably on the originating unit's ability to make a decision
    B. *good*, chiefly because the department's public image is likely to be improved when people see it as trying to save money and speed up its processes
    C. *poor*, chiefly because a letter or document prepared in final form represents an investment of department time and effort and should go out only as a perfect finished product
    D. *good*, chiefly because the document may be important, and sending it back for retyping may delay it too long to achieve its purpose

12.____

13. Suppose that one of the office machines in your unit is badly in need of replacement.
    Of the following, the MOST important reason for postponing immediate purchase of a new machine would be that
    A. a later model of the machine is expected on the market in a few months
    B. the new machine is more expensive than the old machine
    C. the operator of the present machine will have to be instructed by the manufacturer in the operation of the new machine
    D. the employee operating the old machine is not complaining

13.____

14. To avoid cutting off parts of letters when using an automatic letter opener, it is BEST to
    A. arrange all of the letters so that the addresses are right side up
    B. hold the envelopes up to the light to make sure their contents have not settled to the side that is to be opened
    C. strike the envelopes against a table or desktop several times so that the contents of all the envelopes settle to one side
    D. check the enclosures periodically to make sure that the machine has not been cutting into them

15. Of the following, the BEST reason for setting up a partitioned work area for the typists in our office is that
    A. an uninterrupted flow of work among the typists will be possible
    B. complaints about ventilation and lighting will be reduced
    C. the first-line supervisor will have more direct control over the typists
    D. the noise of the typewriters will be less disturbing to other workers

16. From the viewpoint of use of a typewriter to fill in a form, the MOST important design factor to consider is
    A. standard spacing
    B. box headings
    C. serial numbering
    D. vertical guide lines

17. Requests to repair office equipment which appears to be unsafe should be given priority MAINLY because, if repairs are delayed,
    A. there may be injuries to staff
    B. there may be further deterioration of the equipment
    C. work flow may be interrupted
    D. the cost of repair may increase

18. A clerk is asked to complete two assignments – transcribe a handwritten business letter and create a spreadsheet. Which two computer programs would the clerk use?
    A. Microsoft Word and Microsoft Excel
    B. Microsoft Word and Microsoft PowerPoint
    C. Google Docs and Google Chrome
    D. Adobe Reader and Microsoft PowerPoint

19. Generally, the actual floor space occupied by a standard letter-size office file cabinet, when closed, is MOST NEARLY
    A. ½ square foot
    B. 3 square feet
    C. 7 square feet
    D. 11 square feet

20. Suppose a clerk under your supervision accidentally opens a personal letter while handling office mail.
    Under such circumstances, you should tell the clerk to put the letter back into the envelope and
    A. take the letter to the person to whom it belongs and make sure he understands that the clerk did not read it
    B. try to seal the envelope so it won't appear to have been opened

C. write on the envelope "Sorry – opened by mistake," and put his initials on it
D. write on the envelope "Sorry – opened by mistake," but not put his initials on it

21. Standard forms frequently call for entries on them to be printed.
The MAIN reason for this practice is that printing, as compared to writing, is GENERALLY
    A. more compact
    B. more legal
    C. more legible
    D. easier to do

22. After a stenographer types a letter which has been dictated, the finished letter should be carefully read for errors.
If he dictator follows the procedure of carefully reading each transcribed letter, a stenographer, under your supervision, should, unless you instruct her otherwise
    A. not take time to proofread transcribed letters
    B. continue to carefully proofread transcribed letters
    C. review transcribed letters for meaning rather than for errors in typing or transcription
    D. review transcribed letters for errors in typing rather than for errors in transcription

23. In transcribing a letter, the secretary notes that the dictator said, "The series of conferences are planned to be relevant to today's problems." In such a case, the secretary should
    A. type the sentence as it appears in the notes
    B. check with the dictator to see whether he would prefer a different grammatical construction
    C. change the noun so that it is correct
    D. revise the sentence as much as necessary to make it read better

24. Of the following, the BEST procedure for your staff to follow in transcribing several letters that were dictated is to
    A. transcribe first the letters that are most difficult so that they can return immediately to the dictator with any questions
    B. read through the notes for each letter to be sure they have all the information needed before preparing the transcript
    C. transcribe first those letters that are shortest and simplest in order to get them out of the way
    D. read all the notes aloud to a co-worker to see whether they sound right

25. In typing long letters, which of the following is generally considered the LEAST desirable practice?
    A. Numbering the second and succeeding pages of the letter
    B. Typing a single line of a new paragraph as the last line of a page
    C. Dividing a word at the end of a line of typing
    D. Typing the name of the recipient of the letter on the second and succeeding pages

KEY (CORRECT ANSWERS)

1.	C	11.	D
2.	D	12.	B
3.	D	13.	A
4.	B	14.	C
5.	C	15.	D
6.	A	16.	A
7.	D	17.	A
8.	A	18.	A
9.	B	19.	B
10.	C	20.	C

21. C
22. B
23. B
24. B
25. B

TEST 2

DIRECTIONS: Each question or incomplete statement is followed by several suggested answers or completions. Select the one that BEST answers the question or completes the statement. *PRINT THE LETTER OF THE CORRECT ANSWER IN THE SPACE AT THE RIGHT.*

1. The use of a microfilm system for information storage and retrieval would make the MOST sense in an office where
   A. a great number of documents must be kept available for permanent reference
   B. documents are ordinarily kept on file for less than six months
   C. filing is a minor and unimportant part of the office work
   D. most of the records on file are working forms on which additional entries are frequently made

   1._____

2. Of the following concepts, the one which CANNOT be represented suitably by a pie chart is
   A. percent shares
   B. shares in absolute units
   C. time trends
   D. successive totals over time, with their shares

   2._____

3. A pictogram is ESSENTIALLY another version of a(n) _____ chart.
   A. plain bar   B. component bar
   C. pie   D. area

   3._____

4. A time series for a certain cost is presented in a graph. It is drawn so that the vertical (cost) axis starts at a point well above zero. This is a legitimate method of presentation for some purposes, but it may have the effect of
   A. hiding fixed components of the cost
   B. exaggerating changes which, in actual amounts, may be insignificant
   C. minimizing variable components of the cost
   D. impairing correlation analysis

   4._____

5. Certain budgetary data may be represented by bar, area, or volume charts. Which one of the following BEST expressed the most appropriate order of usefulness?
   A. Descends from bar to volume and area charts, the last two being about the same
   B. Descends from volume to area, to bar charts
   C. Depends on the nature of the data presented
   D. Descends from bar to area to volume charts

   5._____

6. One weekend, you develop a painful infection in one hand. You know that your typing speed will be much slower than normal and the likelihood of your making mistakes will be increased.
   Of the following, the BEST course of action for you to take in this situation is to
   A. report to work as scheduled and do your typing assignments as best you can without complaining
   B. report to work as scheduled and ask your co-workers to divide your typing assignments until your hand heals
   C. report to work as scheduled and ask your supervisor for non-typing assignments until your hand heals
   D. call in sick and remain on medical leave until your hand is completely healed so that you can perform your normal duties

7. When filling out a departmental form during an interview concerning a citizen complaint, an interviewer should know the purpose of each question that he asks the citizen. For such information to be supplied by your department is
   A. *advisable*, because the interviewer may lose interest in the job if he is not fully informed about the questions he has to ask
   B. *inadvisable*, because the interviewer may reveal the true purpose of the questions to the citizens
   C. *advisable*, because the interviewer might otherwise record superficial or inadequate answers if he does not fully understand the questions
   D. *inadvisable*, because the information obtained through the form may be of little importance to the interviewer

8. The one of the following which is the BEST reason for placing the date and time of receipt on incoming mail is that this procedure
   A. aids the filing of correspondence in alphabetical order
   B. fixes responsibility for promptness in answering correspondence
   C. indicates that the mail has been checked for the presence of a return address
   D. makes it easier to distribute the main in sequence

9. Which one of the following is the FIRST step that you should take when filing a document by subject?
   A. Arrange related documents by date with the latest date in front
   B. Check whether the document has been released for filing
   C. Cross-reference the document if necessary
   D. Determine the category under which the document will be filed

10. The one of the following which is NOT generally employed to keep track of frequently used material requiring future attention is a
    A. card tickler file   B. dated follow-up folder
    C. periodic transferal of records   D. signal folder

11. Which one of the following is NOT a useful filing practice?
    A. Filing active records in the most accessible parts of the file cabinet
    B. Filing a file drawer to capacity in order to save space
    C. Gluing small documents to standard-size paper before filing
    D. Using different colored labels for various filing categories

12. The one of the following cases in which you would NOT place a special notation in the left margin of a letter that you have typed is when
    A. one of the copies is intended for someone other than the addressee of the letter
    B. you enclose a flyer with the letter
    C. you sign your superior's name to the letter, at his or her request
    D. the letter refers to something being sent under separate cover

13. Suppose that you accidentally cut a letter or enclosure as you are opening an envelope with a paper knife. The one of the following that you should do FIRST is to
    A. determine whether the document is important
    B. clip or staple the pieces together and process as usual
    C. mend the cut document with transparent tape
    D. notify the sender that the communication was damaged and request another copy

14. It is generally advisable to leave at least six inches of working space in a file drawer. This procedure is MOST useful in
    A. decreasing the number of filing errors
    B. facilitating the sorting of documents and folders
    C. maintaining a regular program of removing inactive records
    D. preventing folders and papers from being torn

15. Of the following, the MOST important reason to sort large volumes of documents before filing is that sorting
    A. decreases the need for cross-referencing
    B. eliminates the need to keep the filing up-to-date
    C. prevents overcrowding of the file drawers
    D. saves time and energy in filing

16. When typing a preliminary draft of a report, the one of the following which you should generally NOT do is to
    A. erase typing errors and deletions rather than "X"ing them out
    B. leave plenty of room at the top, bottom, and sides of each page
    C. make only the number of copies that you are asked to make
    D. type double or triple space

17. When printing a 500-page office manual, the most efficient method is to use which of the following office machines?   17._____
    A. Inkjet printer
    B. Copy machine
    C. Word processor
    D. All-in-one scanner/fax/copier

18. When typing name or titles on a roll of folder labels, the one of the following which it is MOST important to do is to type the caption   18._____
    A. as it appears son the papers to be placed in the folder
    B. in capital letters
    C. in exact indexing or filing order
    D. so that it appears near the bottom of the folder tab when the label is attached

19. The MOST important reason for having color cartridges on hand for an office copier even though most prints are black and white is because   19._____
    A. color ink is used for all copies
    B. some copiers or printers will not print black and white if any of the color cartridges are empty
    C. black ink is cheaper when purchasing along with color cartridges
    D. lack of color ink can cause copier malfunctions

20. All of the following pertain to the formatting of word-processing documents EXCEPT   20._____
    A. headers and footers
    B. rows and columns
    C. indents and page breaks
    D. alignment and justified type

KEY (CORRECT ANSWERS)

1.	A	11.	B
2.	C	12.	C
3.	A	13.	C
4.	B	14.	D
5.	D	15.	D
6.	C	16.	A
7.	C	17.	B
8.	B	18.	C
9.	B	19.	B
10.	C	20.	B

TENANT'S RIGHTS

CONTENTS

INTRODUCTION 1

LEASES
    What Is a Lease? 1
    Renewal Leases. 2
    Month-to-Month Tenants 2

RENT
    Rent Charges... 2
    Rent Overcharges 3
    Rent Security Deposits. 3

LEASE SUCCESSION OR TERMINATION
    Subletting or Assigning Leases 4
    Lease Succession Rights 5
    Senior Citizen Lease Terminations. 6
    Lease Terminations for Military Personnel 6
    Eviction 6-7

HABITABILITY AND REPAIRS
    Warranty of Habitability 7
    Landlords' Duty of Repair 8
    Lead Paint 8

SAFETY
    Crime Prevention 8
    Entrance Door Locks and Intercoms... 8
    Lobby Attendant Service... 8
    Elevator Mirrors.. 9
    Individual Locks, Peepholes and Mail 9
    Smoke Detectors 9
    Window Guards 9

TENANT'S PERSONAL RIGHTS
    Tenants' Organizations. 9
    Retaliation... 10
    Right to Privacy... 10
    Discrimination 10
    Harassment 10

UTILITY SERVICES
    Heating Season 11
    Truth in Heating... 11
    Continuation of Utility Service 11
    Oil Payments.. 11

CONTENTS (Continued)

FINDING AN APARTMENT
    Real Estate Brokers 11
    Apartment Information Vendors and Listing Agencies 12

OTHER PROVISIONS
    Apartment Sharing 12
    Pets 12
    Special Types of Housing 12-13

TENANT'S RIGHTS GUIDE

INTRODUCTION

This guide highlights some of the principal rights of residential tenants in this state. These rights are protected by a variety of Federal, State and local laws. In addition, those areas of the State which are subject to rent stabilization, rent control or other rent regulation, may have special rules applicable to certain dwellings. For example, rent stabilization laws apply in New York City and in certain communities in Nassau, Rockland and Westchester counties. Tenants are advised to consult a lawyer regarding particular situations of concern to them.

LEASES

WHAT IS A LEASE?

A lease is a contract between a landlord and tenant which contains the terms and conditions of the rental. It cannot be changed while it is in effect unless both parties agree. Leases for apartments which are not rent stabilized may be oral or written. However, to avoid disputes the parties may wish to enter into a written agreement. An oral lease for more than one year cannot be legally enforced. (General Obligations Law §5-701)

At a minimum, leases should specify the names and addresses of the parties, the amount and due dates of the rent, the duration of the rental, the conditions of occupancy, and the rights and obligations of both parties. Except where the law provides otherwise, a landlord may rent on such terms and conditions as are agreed to by the parties.

Leases must use words with common and everyday meanings and must be clear and coherent. Sections of leases must be appropriately captioned and the print must be large enough to read easily. (General Obligations Law §5-702; C.P.L.R. §4544)

Lease provisions which exempt landlords from liability for injuries to persons or property caused by the landlord's negligence or that of his employees - are null and void. Further, a lease provision that waives the tenant's right to a jury trial in any lawsuit brought by either of the parties against the other for personal injury or property damage is also null and void. (General Obligations Law §5-321; Real Property Law §259-c)

If the court finds a lease or any lease clause to have been unconscionable at the time it was made, the court may refuse to enforce the lease or the clause in question. (Real Property Law §235-c) A lease provision which requires a tenant to pledge his/her household furniture as security for rent is void. (Real Property Law §231)

Tenants protected by rent stabilization have the right to either a one or two year lease when they move into an apartment except under certain circumstances such as, for example, when the apartment is not used as the tenant's primary residence. Rent stabilized tenants must also be given a rent stabilization lease rider, prepared by the New York State Division of Housing and Community Renewal ("DHCR"), which summarizes their rights under the law and provides specific information on how the vacancy rent was calculated. For certain luxury apartments, a landlord may seek DHCR approval to deregulate the rent to be charged.

New York City rent stabilized tenants are entitled to receive from their landlords a fully executed copy of their signed lease within 30 days of the landlord's receipt of the lease signed by the tenant. The lease's beginning and ending dates must be stated. (Rent Stabilization Code ("RSC") §2522.5)

RENEWAL LEASES

Except for rent-regulated apartments, a tenant may only renew the lease with the consent of the landlord. A lease may contain an automatic renewal clause. In such case, the landlord must give the tenant advance notice of the existence of this clause between 15 and 30 days before the tenant is required to notify the landlord of an intention not to renew the lease. (General Obligations Law §5-905)

The renewal leases for rent stabilized tenants must be on the same terms and conditions as the prior lease and rent increases, if any, are limited by law but may provide for a rent increase according to rates permitted by the Rent Guidelines Board. Rent stabilized tenants may choose either a one-year or a two-year renewal lease. For New York City rent-stabilized tenants, the landlord must give written notice to the rent-stabilized tenant of the right to renewal no more than 150 days and not less than 120 days prior to the end of the lease. After the notice of renewal is given, the tenant has 60 days in which to accept. If the tenant does not accept the renewal offer within the prescribed time, the landlord may refuse to renew the lease and seek to evict the tenant through court proceedings.

MONTH-TO-MONTH TENANTS

Tenants who do not have leases and pay rent on a monthly basis are called "month-to-month" tenants. In localities without rent regulations, tenants who stay past the end of a lease are treated as month-to-month tenants if the landlord accepts their rent. (Real Property Law §232-c)

A month-to-month tenancy outside New York City may be terminated by either party by giving at least one month's notice before the expiration of the term. For example, if the rent is due on the first of each month, the landlord must inform the tenant by September 30th before the October rent is due that he wants the tenant to move out by November 1st. The termination notice need not specify why the landlord seeks possession of the apartment. Such notice does not automatically allow the landlord to evict the tenant. A landlord may raise the rent of a month-to-month tenant with the consent of the tenant. If the tenant does not consent, however, the landlord can terminate the tenancy by giving appropriate notice. (Real Property Law §232-b)

In New York City, the landlord must serve the tenant with a written termination giving 30 days notice before the expiration of the term. The notice must state that the landlord elects to terminate the tenancy and that refusal to vacate will lead to eviction proceedings. (Real Property Law §232-a)

RENT

RENT CHARGES

Where an apartment is not subject to rent stabilization or rent control or other rent regulation, a landlord is free to charge any rent agreed upon by the parties. If the apartment is subject to such rent regulation, the rent and subsequent rent increases are set by law. A tenant may challenge the regulated rent with the DHCR. If the challenge is upheld, DHCR will order a refund of any overcharges plus interest and, where appropriate, it may assess penalties.

Landlords of rent stabilized buildings may seek rent increases for certain types of building-wide major capital improvements (MCI), such as the replacement of a boiler, and for new services, new equipment or improvements to an apartment in accordance with the law and regulations. Under certain circumstances, a landlord may also apply for a hardship rent increase.

Landlords must provide tenants with a written receipt when rent is paid in cash, a money order, a cashier's check or in any form other than the personal check of a tenant. Where a tenant pays the rent by personal check, (s)he may request in writing a rent receipt from the landlord. The receipt must state the payment date, the amount, the period for which the rent was paid, and the apartment number. The receipt must be signed by the person receiving the payment and state his or her title. (Real Property Law §235-e)

It is illegal for any person to require a prospective tenant to pay a bonus -commonly called "key money" - above the lawful rent and security deposit - for preference in renting a vacant apartment. (Penal Law 180.55) Key money is not to be confused with fees that may be legally charged by a licensed real estate broker. (See the section below on "Real Estate Brokers")

RENT OVERCHARGES

In New York City and certain communities in Nassau, Rockland and Westchester counties where rent stabilization laws apply, the landlord may not charge more than the legal-regulated rent. Under the housing law, landlords must register each rent-stabilized apartment wit DHCR and provide tenants annually with a copy of the registration statement. Tenants may also get a copy of the rent history for their apartment directly from DHCR. A tenant may only challenge rents and collect any overcharges going back four years from the tenant's filing a complaint. The tenant is also entitled to recover interest, plus reasonable costs and attorney's fees, for the overcharge proceeding.

In addition, if the overcharge is willful, the landlord is liable for a penalty of three times the amount of the overcharge. The penalty includes the amount of the overcharge itself. The landlord has the burden of proving the overcharge is not willful. This treble damages penalty is limited to two years. Contact DHCR if you believe you are being overcharged.

RENT SECURITY DEPOSITS

Virtually all leases require tenants to give their landlords a security deposit. The security deposit is usually one month's rent. The landlord must return the security deposit, less any lawful deduction, to the tenant at the end of the lease or within a reasonable time thereafter. A landlord may use the security deposit: (a) as reimbursement for the reasonable cost of repairs beyond normal wear and tear, if the tenant damages the apartment; or (b) as reimbursement for any unpaid rent.

Landlords, regardless of the number of units in the building, must treat the deposits as trust funds belonging to their tenants and they may not co-mingle deposits with their own money. Landlords of buildings with six or more apartments must put all security deposits in New York bank accounts earning interest at the prevailing rate. Each tenant must be informed in writing of the bank's name and address and the amount of the deposit. Landlords are entitled to annual administrative expenses of 1% of the deposit. All other interest earned on the deposits belongs to the tenants. Tenants must be given the option of having this interest paid to them annually, applied to rent, or paid at the end of the lease term. If the building has fewer than six apartments, a landlord who voluntarily places the security deposits in an interest bearing bank account must also follow these rules. For example: A tenant pays a security deposit of $400. The landlord places the deposit in an interest bearing bank account paying 2.5%. At the end of the year the account will have earned interest of $10.00. The tenant is entitled to $6.00 and the landlord may retain $4.00, 1% of the deposit, as an administrative fee.

If the building is sold, the landlord must transfer all security deposits to the new owner within five days, or return the security deposits to the tenants. Landlords must notify the tenants, by registered or certified mail, of the name and address of the new owner. Purchasers of rent-stabilized buildings are directly responsible to tenants for the return of security deposits and any interest. This responsibility exists whether or not the new owner received the security deposits from the former landlord.

Purchasers of rent-controlled buildings or buildings containing six or more apartments where tenants have written leases are directly responsible to tenants for the return of security deposits and interest in cases where the purchaser has "actual knowledge" of the security deposits. The law defines specifically when a new owner is deemed to have "actual knowledge" of the security deposits.

When problems arise, tenants should first try to resolve them with the landlord before taking other action. If a dispute cannot be resolved, tenants may contact the nearest local office of the Attorney General.

LEASE SUCCESSION OR TERMINATION

SUBLETTING OR ASSIGNING LEASES

Subletting and assignment are methods of transferring the tenant's legal interest in an apartment to another person. A sublet transfers less than the tenant's entire interest while an assignment transfers the entire interest. A tenant's right to assign the lease is much more restricted than the right to sublet.

A tenant may not assign the lease without the landlord's written consent. The landlord may withhold consent without cause. If the landlord reasonably refuses consent, the tenant cannot assign and is not entitled to be released from the lease. If the landlord unreasonably refuses consent, the tenant is entitled to be released from the lease after 30 days notice.

Tenants with leases who live in buildings with four or more apartments have the right to sublet with the landlord's advance consent. The landlord cannot unreasonably withhold consent. If the landlord consents to the sublet, the tenant remains liable to the landlord for the obligations of the lease. If the landlord denies the sublet on reasonable grounds, the tenant cannot sublet and the landlord is not required to release the tenant from the lease. If the landlord denies the sublet on unreasonable grounds, the tenant may sublet. If a lawsuit results, the tenant may recover court costs and attorney's fees if a judge rules that the landlord denied the sublet in bad faith.

These steps must be followed by tenants wishing to sublet:
1. The tenant must send a written request to the landlord by certified mail, return-receipt requested. The request must contain the following information: (a) the length of the sublease; (b) the name, home and business address of the proposed subtenant; (c) the reason for subletting; (d) the tenant's address during the sublet; (e) the written consent of any co-tenant or guarantor; (f) a copy of the proposed sublease together with a copy of the tenant's own lease, if available.
2. Within 10 days after the mailing of this request, the landlord may ask the tenant for additional information to help make a decision. Any request for additional information may not be unduly burdensome.
3. Within 30 days after the mailing of the tenant's request to sublet or the additional information requested by the landlord, whichever is later, the landlord must send

the tenant a notice of consent, or if consent is denied, the reasons for denial. A landlord's failure to send this written notice is considered consent to sublet.
4. A sublet or assignment which does not comply with the law may be grounds for eviction.

In addition to these sublet rules, there are additional requirements limited to rent stabilized tenants. These rules include the following:

- The rent charged to the subtenant cannot exceed the stabilized rent plus a 10% surcharge payable to the tenant for a furnished sublet. Additionally, the stabilized rent payable to the owner, effective upon the date of subletting, may be increased by a "sublet allowance" equal to the vacancy allowance then in effect. A subtenant who is overcharged may file a complaint with DHCR or may sue the prime tenant in court to recover any overcharge plus treble damages, interest, and attorneys' fees (RSC §2525.6(e))
- The prime tenant must establish that at all times he/she has maintained the apartment as a primary residence and intends to reoccupy it at the end of the sublet.
- The prime tenant, not the subtenant, retains the rights to a renewal lease and any rights resulting from a co-op conversion. The term of a sublease may extend beyond the term of the prime tenant's lease. The tenant may not sublet for more than two years within any four-year period. (Real Property Law §226-b, RSC §2525.6)
- Rent stabilized tenants who sublet their apartments should note that the Rent Stabilization Code published on December 20, 2000 created a new subdivision setting forth what constitutes a tenant's primary residence. Section 9: 9 NYCRR §2520.6(u) states in part that a rent stabilized tenant subletting his or her apartment may now permit a landlord to seek possession of the subject premises on the basis of non-primary residence.

LEASE SUCCESSION RIGHTS

Family members living in an apartment not covered by rent control or rent stabilization generally have no right to succeed a tenant who dies or permanently vacates the premises. The rights of a "family member" living in a rent controlled or rent stabilized apartment to succeed a tenant of record who dies or permanently vacates are covered by DHCR Regulations.

Under these regulations, a "family member" is defined as husband, wife, son, daughter, stepson, stepdaughter, father, mother, stepfather, stepmother, brother, sister, grandfather, grandmother, grandson, granddaughter, father-in-law, mother-in-law, son-in-law or daughter-in-law of the tenant; or any other person residing with the tenant in the apartment as a primary resident who can prove emotional and financial commitment, and interdependence between such person and the tenant.

A family member would succeed to the rights of the tenant of record upon the tenant's permanent departure or death, provided the family member lived with such a primary resident either (1) for not less than two years (one year in the case of senior citizens who are 62 years or older, and disabled persons) or (2) from the commencement of the tenancy or the relationship (if the tenancy or relationship were less than two years or one year old, as the case may be). (RSC §2523.5)

Remaining family members living in government involved housing such as a public development; or in an apartment owned by the local municipality; or in an apartment where the prime tenant had some type of Section 8 Rental Assistance; and where the named tenant of record has died or moved out, may also have the right to succeed to that tenant's leasehold and/or rent subsidy. Family members seeking succession rights in these circumstances must ascertain the applicable federal and municipal regulations as well as the local public housing authority rules to determine if they might meet the eligibility requirements. Under federal regulations, persons alleging they are remaining family members of tenant family are entitled to a grievance hearing before eviction if they have a colorable claim to such status.

SENIOR CITIZEN LEASE TERMINATIONS

Tenants or their spouses living with them, who are sixty-two years or older, or who will attain such age during the term of their leases, are entitled to terminate their leases if they relocate to an adult care facility, a residential health care facility, subsidized low-income housing, or other senior citizen housing.

When such tenants give notice of their opportunity to move into one of the above facilities, the landlord must release the tenant from liability to pay rent for the balance of the lease and adjust any payments made in advance.

Senior citizens who wish to avail themselves of this option must do so by written notice to the landlord. The termination date must be effective no earlier than thirty days after the date on which the next rental payment (after the notice is delivered) is due. The notice is deemed delivered five days after mailing. The written notice must include documentation of admission or pending admission to one of the above mentioned facilities. For example, a senior citizen mails a notice to the landlord of his or her intention to terminate the lease on April 5; the notice is deemed received April 10. Since the next rental payment (after April 10) is due May 1, the earliest lease termination date will be effective June 1.

Anyone who interferes with the tenant's or his or her spouse's removal of personal effects, clothing, furniture or other personal property from the premises to be vacated will be guilty of a misdemeanor.

Owners or lessors of a facility of a unit into which a senior citizen is entitled to move after terminating a lease, must advise such tenant, in the admission application form, of the tenant's rights under the law. (Real Property Law §227-a.)

LEASE TERMINATIONS FOR MILITARY PERSONNEL

Individuals entering or called to active duty in the military service may terminate a residential lease if: (1) the lease was executed by the service member before he/she entered active duty; and (2) the leased premises have been occupied by the member or his/her dependents. Any such lease may be terminated by written notice delivered to the landlord at any time following the beginning of military service. Termination of a lease requiring monthly payments is not effective until 30 days after the first date on which the next rent is due. For example, if rent is due on the first day of the month, and notice is mailed on January 1, then rent is next due on the first of February and the effective date of lease termination is the first of March (N.Y. Military Law §309).

EVICTION

Following appropriate notice, a landlord may bring a summary non-payment court proceeding to evict a tenant who fails to pay the agreed rent when due and to recover outstanding rent. A landlord may also bring a summary holdover eviction proceeding if, for example, a tenant significantly violates a substantial obligation under the lease, such as using the premises for illegal purposes, committing or permitting a nuisance, or staying beyond the lease term without permission. (Real Property Actions Proceedings Law ("RPAPL")§711)

You can be legally evicted only after the landlord has brought a court proceeding and obtained a judgement of possession. An eviction notice can be sent to you if: you signed an agreement (stipulation) with the landlord in court granting the landlord a final judgement and you did not fulfill the terms of the agreement; or you had a trial and the judge ruled in the landlord's favor; or you did not appear in court to answer court papers (petition) that the landlord sent you. Only a sheriff, marshal or constable can carry out a court ordered warrant to evict a tenant. (RPAPL §749) A landlord may not take the law into his/her own hands and evict a tenant by use of force or unlawful means. For example, a landlord cannot use threats of violence, remove a tenant's possessions, lock the tenant out of the apartment, or willfully discontinue essential services such as water or heat. (Real Property Law §235) When a tenant is evicted, the landlord may not retain the tenant's personal belongings or furniture.

A tenant who is put out of his/her apartment in a forcible or unlawful manner is entitled to recover triple damages in a legal action against the wrongdoer. Landlords in New York City who use illegal methods to force a tenant to move are also subject to both criminal and civil penalties. Further, the tenant is entitled to be restored to occupancy. (RPAPL §713, §853)

It is wise to consult an attorney to protect your legal rights if your landlord seeks possession of your apartment. Never ignore legal papers.

HABITABILITY AND REPAIRS

WARRANTY OF HABITABILITY

Tenants are entitled to a livable, safe and sanitary apartment. Lease provisions inconsistent with this right are illegal. Failure to provide heat or hot water on a regular basis, or to rid an apartment of insect infestation are examples of a violation of this warranty. Public areas of the building are also covered by the warranty of habitability. The warranty of habitability also applies to cooperative apartments, but not to condominiums. Any uninhabitable condition caused by the tenant or persons under his direction or control does not constitute a breach of the warranty of habitability. In such a case, it is the responsibility of the tenant to remedy the condition. (Real Property Law §235-b)

If a landlord breaches the warranty, the tenant may sue for a rent reduction. The tenant may also withhold rent, but in response, the landlord may sue the tenant for nonpayment of rent. In such a case, the tenant may countersue for breach of the warranty.

Rent reductions may be ordered if a court finds that the landlord violated the warranty of habitability. The reduction is computed by subtracting from the actual rent the estimated value of the apartment without the essential services.

A landlord's liability for damages is limited when the failure to provide services is the result of a union-wide building workers' strike. However, a court may award damages to a tenant equal to a share of the landlord's net savings because of the strike.

Landlords will be liable for lack of services caused by a strike when they have not made a good faith attempt, where practicable, to provide services.

In emergencies, tenants may make necessary repairs and deduct reasonable repair costs from the rent. For example, when a landlord has been notified that a door lock is broken and willfully neglects to repair it, the tenant may hire a locksmith and deduct the cost from the rent. Tenants should keep receipts for such repairs.

LANDLORDS' DUTY OF REPAIR

Landlords of buildings with three or more apartments must keep the apartments and the buildings' public areas in "good repair" and clean and free of vermin, garbage or other offensive material. Landlords are required to maintain electrical, plumbing, sanitary, heating and ventilating systems and appliances landlords install, such as refrigerators and stoves in good and safe working order. Tenants should bring complaints to the attention of their local housing officials. (Multiple Dwelling Law (MDL) 78 and 80; Multiple Residence Law (MRL) §174. The MDL applies to cities with a population of 325,000 or more and the MRL applies to cities with less than 325,000 and to all towns and villages.)

LEAD PAINT

Landlords of apartments in multiple dwellings in New York City where a child 6 years old or younger lives must protect against the possibility that children will be poisoned by peeling of dangerous lead based paint. Landlords must remove or cover apartment walls and other areas where lead based paint was used in the apartment if the building was built prior to January 1, 1960. (NYC Health Code §173.14) Landlords must provide all tenants with a pamphlet prepared by the federal Environmental Protection Agency which warns the tenants of the hazards of lead based paint and a disclosure form advising what the landlord knows about the presence of lead based paint in the apartment and building.

SAFETY

CRIME PREVENTION

Landlords are required to take minimal precautions to protect against foreseeable criminal harm. For example, tenants who are victims of crimes in their building or apartment, and who are able to prove that the criminal was an intruder and took advantage of the fact that the entrance to the building was negligently maintained by the landlord, may be able to recover damages from the landlord.

ENTRANCE DOOR LOCKS AND INTERCOMS

Multiple dwellings which were built or converted to such use after January 1, 1968 must have automatic self-closing and self-locking doors at all entrances. These doors must be kept locked at all times - except when an attendant is on duty.
If this type of building contains eight or more apartments it must also have a two-way voice intercom system from each apartment to the front door and tenants must be able to "buzz" open the entrance door for visitors.
Multiple dwellings built or converted to such use prior to January 1,1968 also must have self-locking doors and a two-way intercom system if requested by a majority of the tenants. Landlords may recover from tenants the cost of providing this equipment. (Multiple Dwelling Law 50-a)

LOBBY ATTENDANT SERVICE

Tenants of multiple dwellings with eight or more apartments, are entitled to maintain a lobby attendant service for their safety and security, whenever any attendant provided by the landlord is not on duty. (Multiple Dwelling Law §50-c)

ELEVATOR MIRRORS

There must be a mirror in each self-service elevator in multiple dwellings so that people may see - prior to entering - if anyone is already in the elevator. (Multiple Dwelling Law §51-b; NYC Admin. Code §27-2042)

INDIVIDUAL LOCKS, PEEPHOLES AND MAIL

Tenants in multiple dwellings can install and maintain their own locks on their apartment entrance doors in addition to the lock supplied by the landlord. The lock may be no more than three inches in circumference, and tenants must provide their landlord with a duplicate key upon request.

The landlord must provide a peephole in the entrance door of each apartment. Landlords of multiple dwellings in New York City must also install a chain-door guard on the entrance door to each apartment, so as to permit partial opening of the door. (Multiple Dwelling Law §51-c; NYC Admin. Code §27-2043)

United States Postal regulations require landlords of buildings containing three or more apartments to provide secure mail boxes for each apartment unless the management has arranged to distribute the mail to each apartment. Landlords must keep the mail boxes and locks in good repair.

SMOKE DETECTORS

Outside New York City and in Buffalo, each apartment in a multiple dwelling (three or more apartments) must be equipped by the landlord with at least one smoke detector that is clearly audible in any sleeping area. (Multiple Residence Law §15; Buffalo Code Ch. 395)

Landlords of multiple dwellings in New York City must also install one or more approved smoke detectors in each apartment near each room used for sleeping. Tenants may be asked to reimburse the owner up to $10.00 for the cost of purchasing and installing each battery-operated detector. During the first year of use, landlords must repair or replace any broken detector if its malfunction is not the tenant's fault. Tenants should test their detectors frequently to make sure they work properly. (NYC Admin. Code §27-2045, §27-2046)

WINDOW GUARDS

Landlords of multiple dwellings in New York City must install government approved window guards in each window in any apartment where a child ten years old or younger lives. Tenants are required to have such guards installed. In other cases, landlords are required to install window guards provided the tenant requests them. Windows giving access to fire escapes are excluded. Protective guards must also be installed on the windows of all public hallways. Landlords must give tenants an annual notice about their rights to window guards and must provide this information in a lease rider. Rent controlled and stabilized tenants may be charged for these guards. (NYC Health Code §131.15)

TENANT'S PERSONAL RIGHTS

TENANTS' ORGANIZATIONS

Tenants have a legal right to organize. They may form, join, and participate in tenants' organizations for the purpose of protecting their rights. Landlords may not harass or penalize tenants who exercise this right. (Real Property Law §230)

RETALIATION

Landlords are prohibited from harassing or retaliating against tenants who exercise their rights. For example, landlords may not seek to evict tenants solely because tenants (a) make good faith complaints to a government agency about violations of any health or safety laws; or (b) take good faith actions to protect rights under their lease; or (c) participate in tenants' organizations. Tenants may collect damages from landlords who violate this law, which applies to all rentals except owner-occupied dwellings with fewer than four units. (Real Property Law §223-b)

RIGHT TO PRIVACY

Tenants have the right to privacy within their apartments. A landlord, however, may enter a tenant's apartment with reasonable prior notice, and at a reasonable time: (a) to provide necessary or agreed upon repairs or services; or (b) in accordance with the lease; or (c) to show the apartment to prospective purchasers or tenants. In emergencies, such as fires, the landlord may enter the apartment without the tenant's consent. A landlord may not abuse this limited right of entry or use it to harass a tenant. A landlord may not interfere with the installation of cable television facilities. (Public Service Law §228)

DISCRIMINATION

Landlords may not refuse to rent to anyone or renew leases of, or otherwise discriminate against, any person or group of persons because of race, creed, color, national origin, sex, disability, age, marital status or familial status. (Executive Law §296 (5)) In addition, in New York City, tenants are further protected against discrimination with respect to lawful occupation, sexual orientation or immigration status. Aggrieved tenants may complain to the New York City Human Rights Commission. (NYC Admin. Code §8-107(5)(a))

Landlords may not refuse to lease an apartment or discriminate against any person in the terms and conditions of the rental because that person has children living with them. This restriction does not apply to housing units for senior citizens which are subsidized or insured by the federal government or to one- or two-family owner occupied houses or manufactured homes. An aggrieved family may sue for damages against a landlord who violates this law and may recover attorneys fees. (Real Property Law §236)

In addition, a lease may not require that tenants agree to remain childless during their tenancy. (Real Property Law §237)

HARASSMENT

A landlord may not take any action to unlawfully force rent regulated tenants to vacate their apartments or to give up any rights they have under the rent laws. Landlords found guilty of harassment are subject to fines of up to $5,000 for each violation. Tenants may contact DHCR if they believe they are the victims of harassment. Under certain circumstances, harassment can constitute a class E felony. (Penal Law Article §241)

11

UTILITY SERVICES

HEATING SEASON

Heat must be supplied from October 1 through May 31, to tenants in multiple dwellings if: (a) the outdoor temperature falls below 55 degrees Fahrenheit, between 6 A.M. and 10 P.M., each apartment must be heated to a temperature of at least 68 degrees Fahrenheit; (b) the outdoor temperature falls below 40 degrees Fahrenheit, between the hours of 10 P.M. and 6 A.M., each apartment must be heated to a temperature of at least 55 degrees Fahrenheit. (Multiple Dwelling Law §79)

TRUTH IN HEATING

Before signing a lease requiring payment of individual heating and cooling bills, prospective tenants are entitled to receive from the landlord, a complete set or summary of the past two years' bills. These copies must be provided free upon written request. (Energy Law §17-103)

CONTINUATION OF UTILITY SERVICE

When the landlord of a multiple dwelling is delinquent in paying utility bills, the utility must give advance written notice to tenants and to certain government agencies of its intent to discontinue service. Service may not be discontinued if tenants pay the landlord's current bill directly to the utility company. Tenants can deduct these charges from future rent payments. The Public Service Commission can assist tenants with related problems.

If a landlord of a multiple dwelling fails to pay a utility bill and service is discontinued, tenants can receive payment for damages from the landlord. (Real Property Law §235-a; Public Service Law §33)

OIL PAYMENTS

Tenants in oil heated multiple dwellings may contract with an oil dealer, and pay for oil deliveries to their building, when the landlord fails to ensure a sufficient fuel supply. These payments are deductible from rent. Local housing officials have lists of oil dealers who will make fuel deliveries under these circumstances. (Multiple Dwelling Law §302-c; Multiple Residence Law §305-c)

FINDING AN APARTMENT

REAL ESTATE BROKERS

A consumer may retain a real estate broker to find a suitable apartment. New York State licenses real estate brokers and salespersons. Brokers charge a commission for their services which is usually a stated percentage of the first year's rent. The amount of the commission is not set by law and should be negotiated between the parties. The broker must assist the client in finding and obtaining an apartment before a commission may be charged. The fee should not be paid until the client is offered a lease signed by the landlord. Complaints against real estate brokers may be brought to the attention of the New York Department of State. (Real Property Law, Article 12-A)

APARTMENT INFORMATION VENDORS AND LISTING AGENCIES

Businesses that charge a fee for providing information about the location and availability of rental housing must be licensed by the State. The fees charged by these firms may not exceed one month's rent. When the information provided by the firms does not result in a rental, the entire amount of any pre-paid fee, less $15.00, must be returned to the tenant. Criminal prosecution for violations of this law may be brought by the Attorney General. (Real Property Law, Article 12-C)

OTHER PROVISIONS

APARTMENT SHARING

It is unlawful for a landlord to restrict occupancy of an apartment to the named tenant in the lease or to that tenant and immediate family. When the lease names only one tenant, that tenant may share the apartment with immediate family, one additional occupant and the occupant's dependent children, provided that the tenant or the tenant's spouse occupies the premises as their primary residence.

When the lease names more than one tenant, these tenants may share their apartment with immediate family, and, if one of the tenants named in the lease moves out, that tenant may be replaced with another occupant and the dependent children of the occupant. At least one of the tenants named in the lease or that tenant's spouse must occupy the shared apartment as his or her primary residence.

Tenants must inform their landlords of the name of any occupant within 30 days after the occupant has moved into the apartment or within 30 days of a landlord's request for this information. If the tenant named in the lease moves out, the remaining occupant has no right to continue in occupancy without the landlord's express consent. Landlords may limit the total number of people living in any apartment to comply with legal overcrowding standards. (Real Property Law §235-f)

PETS

Tenants may keep pets in their apartments if their lease permits pets or is silent on the subject. Landlords may be able to evict tenants who violate a lease provision prohibiting pets. In multiple dwellings in New York City and Westchester County, a no-pet lease clause is deemed waived where a tenant "openly and notoriously" kept a pet for at least three months and the owner of the building or his agent had knowledge of this fact. However, this protection does not apply where the animal causes damage, is a nuisance, or substantially interferes with other tenants. (NYC Admin. Code §27-2009.1(b); Westchester County Laws, Chapter 694). Tenants who are blind or deaf are permitted to have guide dogs or service dogs regardless of a no-pet clause in their lease. (Civil Rights Law §47)

SPECIAL TYPES OF HOUSING

The rights, duties and responsibilities of *Manufactured Home Park's* owners and tenants are governed by Real Property Law §233, popularly known as the "Manufactured Home Owners Bill of Rights." The DHCR has the authority to enforce compliance with this law.

The rights, duties and responsibilities of *New York City loft owners and tenants are* governed by Multiple Dwelling Law, Article 7-C. The New York City Loft Board has the authority to enforce this law.

The rights, duties and responsibilities of *New York City residential hotel owners and tenants* are governed by the rent stabilization law. The DHCR has the authority to enforce compliance with this law.

Public housing is a federally authorized and funded program in which state-charted public housing authorities develop, own and manage public housing developments. Public housing in New York State is subject to federal, state, and local laws and regulations. See 42 U.S.C. §1437 et seq.; Public Housing Law (statutes); 24 CFR Parts 912-999; and 9 NYCRR §1627 et seq. (regulations). Generally, tenants in government-involved housing are entitled to due process protections which may constrain any action by the landlord. By and large, tenants can not be evicted from their homes without proof of some "good cause" by the landlord where the government is involved in the housing, whether through direct ownership, subsidy or regulation.

TRENDS IN HOUSING

CONTENTS

		Page
I.	The History of Housing	1
II.	Trends in Housing Inspection	4
III.	Role of Health Agencies in Housing	6
IV.	Summary	6

TRENDS IN HOUSING

Members of countless communities throughout America are raising critical questions about the adequacy and effectiveness of local housing code enforcement programs. These critics feel deep concern over the fact that 1966 found "some four million urban families living in homes of such disrepair as to violate decent housing standards." For this reason, they insist everything possible be done to guarantee that present and future inspection efforts lead to rapid and adequate upgrading of the substandard but salvageable housing in each community and that the neighborhoods be made more desirable places in which to live.

In order to meet these demands effectively, inspectors of housing and their supervisors should first acquaint themselves with the origin of public concern about housing problems; the past, present, and new approaches to housing code administration; the expanded role of the inspection function in the neighborhood improvement effort; and the general nature of their role and responsibilities

I. The History of Housing

The first public policies on housing in this country were established during the Colonial period. Many of the early settlers built houses with wooden chimneys and thatched roofs which were the causes of frequent fires. Consequently, several of the colonies passed regulations prohibiting these. One of the first was the Plymouth Colony, which in 1626 passed a law stipulating that new houses should not be thatched but roofed with either board or pale and the like. In 1648 wooden or plastered chimneys were prohibited on new houses in New Amsterdam, and chimneys on existing houses were decreed to be inspected regularly. In Charlestown in 1740, following a disastrous fire, the general assembly passed an act that declared that all buildings should be of brick or stone, that all "tall" wooded houses must be pulled down by 1745, and that the use of wood was to be confined to window frames, shutters, and to exterior work. This law was obviously unenforceable because, as we learn from other publications during that period, more Charlestown houses were made of timber than of brick.

Social control over housing was exerted in other ways. Early settlers in Pennsylvania frequently dug caves out of the banks of the Delaware River and used these as primitive-type dwellings. Some of these shelters were still in use as late as 1687 when the Provincial Council ordered inhabitants to provide for themselves other habitations, in order to have the said caves or houses destroyed. In some New England communities, around the turn of the 18th century, standards were raised considerably higher by local ordinances. In East Greenwich, it had been the custom to build houses 14 feet square with posts 9 feet high; in 1727 the town voted that houses shall be built 18 feet square with-posts 15 feet high with chimneys of stone or brick as before.

During the early days of this country, basic sanitation was very poor, primarily because outdoor privies served as the general means of sewage disposal. The principal problems created by the use of these privies involved their nearness to the streets and their easy accessibility to hogs and goats. In 1652, Boston prohibited the building of privies within 12 feet of the street. The Dutch of New Amsterdam in 1657 prohibited the throwing of rubbish and filth into the streets or canal and required the householders to keep the streets clean and orderly.

After the early Colonial period we pass into an era of very rapid metropolitan growth along the eastern seashore. This growth was due largely to the immigration of people from Europe. Frequently these immigrants arrived without money or jobs and were forced to move in with friends or relatives. This led to severe overcrowding. Most of the information available pertains to New York City, because the situation there was worse than that in any other city in the country. It received the majority of the immigrants, many of whom were unable to move beyond the city. The most serious housing problems began in New York about 1840 when the first tenements were built. These provided such substandard housing and such unhealthy, crowded living conditions that a social reform movement was imminent in New York.

During the early part of the 19th century, the only housing control authority was that vested in the fire wardens, whose objective was to prevent fires, and the health wardens, who were charged with the enforcement of general sanitation. In 1867, with the passing of the Tenement Housing Act, New York City began to face the problem of substandard housing. This law represented the first comprehensive legislation of its kind in this country. The principal features of the act are summarized as follows: for every room occupied for sleeping in a tenement or lodging house, if it does not communicate directly with the external air, a ventilating or transom window to the neighboring room or hall; a proper fire escape on every tenement or lodging house; the roof to be kept in repair and the stairs to have bannisters; water closets or privies – at least one to every twenty occupants for all such houses; after July 1, 1867, permits for occupancy of every cellar not previously occupied as a dwelling; cleansing of every lodging house to the satisfaction of the Board of Health, which is to have access at any time; reporting of all cases of infectious disease to the Board by the owner or his agent; inspection and, if necessary, disinfection of such houses; and vacation of buildings found to be out of repair. There were also regulations governing distances between buildings, heights of rooms, and dimensions of windows. The terms "tenement house," "lodging house," and "cellar" were defined.

Although this act had some beneficial influences on overcrowding, sewage disposal, lighting, and ventilation, it did not correct the evils of crowding on lots and did not provide for adequate ventilation for inner rooms. In 1879, a second tenement act, amending the first, was passed adding restrictions on the amount of lot coverage and providing for a window opening of at least 12 square feet in every room. Several attempts in 1882, 1884, and 1895 were made to amend this original act and provide for occupancy standards, but they were relatively unenforceable. While these numerous acts remedied only slightly the serious problems of the tenements, they did show the city's acknowledgment of the problems. This public acknowledgment, however, was seldom shared by the owners of the tenements, or, in some cases, by the courts. The most famous case, in 1892, involved Trinity Church, at that time one of the largest owners of tenements in New York City. In the case, the City of New York accused Trinity Church of violating provisions of the Act of 1882 by failing to provide running water on every floor of its buildings. A district court levied a fine of $200 against the Church, which in turn appealed to the Court of Common Pleas to have the law set aside as unconstitutional. Incredibly, the court agreed unanimously to uphold the landlord's position, stating there is no evidence nor can the court judicially know that the presence and distribution of water on the several floors will conduce to the health of the occupants ... there is no necessity for legislative compulsion on a landlord to distribute water through the stories of his building; since if tenants require it, self-interest and the rivalry of competition are sufficient to secure it ... now, if it be competent for the legislature to impose an expense upon a landlord in order that tenants be furnished with water in their rooms instead of in the yard or basement, at what point must this police power pause? ... a conclusion contrary to the present decision would involve the essential principle of that species of socialism under the regime of which the individual disappears and is absorbed by a collective being called the 'state', a principle utterly repugnant to the spirit of our political system and necessarily fatal to our form of liberty. Fortunately, 3 years later, the city health department was granted an appeal from the court order, and eventually the constitutionality of the law was upheld.

Jacob A. Riis, Lawrence Veiller, and others did much during this period to champion the cause of better living conditions. Their efforts resulted in the Tenement House Act of 1901, a milestone in housing and an extremely comprehensive document for its time. It began with concise definitions of certain terms that were to become important in court actions. It contained provisions for protection from fire, requiring that every tenement erected thereafter, and exceeding 60 feet in height, should be fireproof. In addition, there were specific provisions regarding fire escapes on both new and existing houses. More light and ventilation were required; coverage was restricted to not more than 70 percent on interior lots and 90 percent on corner lots. There were special provisions governing rear yards, inner courts, and buildings on the same lot with the tenement house. At least one window of specified dimensions was required for every room, including the bathroom. Minimum size of rooms was specified as were certain characteristics for public halls. Significantly included were provisions concerning planning for the individual apartments in order to assure privacy. One of the most important provisions of the Tenement Act was the requirement for running water and water closets in each apartment in new tenement houses. Special attention was given to basements and cellars, the law requiring not only that they be damp-proof but also that permits be obtained before they were occupied. One novel section of this act prohibited the use of any part of the building as a house of prostitution.

The basic principles and methodology established in the Tenement Act of 1901 still underlie much of the housing efforts in New York City today. Philadelphia, a city that can be compared with New York from the standpoint of age, was fortunate to have farsighted leaders in its early stage of development. Since 1909, with the establishment of the Philadelphia Housing Association, the city has had almost continual inspection and improvement.

Although Chicago is approximately two centuries younger than New York, it enacted housing legislation as early as 1889 and health legislation as early as 1881. Regulations on ventilation, light, drainage, and plumbing of dwellings were put into effect in 1896. Many of the structures, however, were built of wood, were dilapidated, and constituted serious fire hazards.

Before 1892, all government involvement in housing was at a local level. In 1892, however, the Federal Government passed a resolution authorizing investigation of slum conditions in cities containing 200,000 or more inhabitants. At that time these included the cities of Baltimore, Boston, Brooklyn, Buffalo, Chicago, Cincinnati, Cleveland, Detroit, Milwaukee, New Orleans, New York, Philadelphia, Pittsburgh, St. Louis, San Francisco, and Washington. Much controversy surrounded the involvement of the Federal Government in housing. The Commissioner of Labor was forced to write an extensive legal opinion concerning the constitutionality of expenditures by the Federal Government in this area. The result was that Congress appropriated only $20,000 to cover the expenses of this project. The lack of funds limited actual investigations to Baltimore, Chicago, New York, and Philadelphia and did not cover housing conditions in toto within these cities. Facts obtained from the investigation were very broad, covering items such as the number of saloons per number of inhabitants, number of arrests, distribution of males and females, proportion of foreign-born inhabitants, degree of illiteracy, kinds of occupations of the residents, conditions of their health, their earnings, and the number of voters.

The 20th century started off rather poorly in the area of housing. No significant housing legislation was passed until 1929 when the New York State legislature passed its Multiple Dwelling Law. This law continued the Tenement Act of New York City but replaced many provisions of the 1901 law with less strict requirements. Other cities and states followed New York State's example and permitted less strict requirements in their codes. This decreased what little emphasis there was in enforcement of building laws so that during the 1920's the cities had worked themselves into a very poor state of housing. Conditions in America declined to such a state by the 30's that President Franklin D. Roosevelt's shocking report to the people was "that one-third of the nation is ill-fed, ill-housed, and ill-clothed." With this the Federal Government launched itself extensively into the field of housing. The first Federal housing law was passed in

1934. One of the purposes of this act was to create a sounder mortgage system through the provision of a permanent system of government insurance for residential mortgages. The Federal Housing Administration was created to carry out the objectives of this act. Many other Federal laws followed: the Veterans Administration becoming involved in guaranteeing of loans, the Home Loan Bank Board, Federal National Mortgage Association, Communities Facilities Administration, Public Housing Administration, and the Public Works Administration. With the U.S. Housing Act of 1937, the Federal Government entered the area of slum clearance and urban renewal, requiring one slum dwelling to be eliminated for every new unit built under the Housing Administration program. It was not until the passage of the Housing Act of 1949 that the Federal Government entered into slum clearance on a comprehensive basis.

The many responsibilities in housing administered by various agencies within the Federal Government proved to be unwieldy. Hence, in 1966 the Department of Housing and Urban Development was created to have prime responsibilities for the Federal Government's involvement in the field of housing.

II. Trends in Housing Inspection

Historically, local provisions for the inspection of housing have been completely inadequate. Usually the function has been split among two or more agencies, and the pertinent code sections have been spread among several local ordinances.

Following the work of C.E.A. Winslow, minimum code standards were made available and resulted in the passing of housing codes. This consolidation of housing requirements resulted in the field of housing inspection. Originally much of the work was devoted to complaint and referral inspections

A Complaint and Referral Inspections

In most communities the housing inspectors are expected to center their efforts primarily on complaint and referral inspections. This approach satisfies the persons making the complaints and referrals and helps improve some of the municipality's substandard housing. However, it does little to bring about general improvements in any section of the community and actually constitutes an inefficient way of using the available inspection manpower because the men have to spend so much time traveling from one area to another. Many supervisors and inspectors realize this unsystematic method not only wastes time but also is an ineffective way of upgrading housing and curbing blight. First, on complaint inspections the inspectors are usually instructed to confine their investigations to the dwelling unit specifically involved unless the general conditions are so bad that an inspection of the entire building is deemed necessary. This means most complaint inspections are piecemeal and do not ordinarily bring entire dwellings up to code standards. Second, even though numerous complaints are unwarranted, inspectors are often given so many to check each day that they do not have time to inspect other obviously substandard houses in the vicinity of those complained about. Consequently, these "rotten apples" are left to spoil the block, while the house that has been improved stands alone.

Too often inspection agencies have found they did not have enough facts on hand about the extent and distribution of the substandard housing in their communities. Thus, they were unable to convince their superiors and the public about the inadequacy of complaint inspections as the major method of uncovering violations and checking residential blight in neighborhoods. It is the consensus of housing officials that area inspections are the most effective way of doing both. Fortunately, in the 1960's, as one city after another began developing the comprehensive community renewal plans provided for in the Housing Act of 1959, this information finally started to become available. It verified the need for systematic inspections on a neighborhood basis. Congress further emphasized the importance of this new approach by including Section 301 in the Housing Act of 1964. This required all cities engaged in urban renewal to have comprehensive area inspection programs in operation by March 1967, and thereafter, in order to remain eligible for national renewal funds.

B Neighborhood Inspection Technique

The area or neighborhood inspection technique is a more recent type of inspection and one which begins to face up to the problems of saving neighborhoods from urban blight. While this is a step forward, it is merely one of several steps required if urban blight and its associated human suffering are to be minimized or controlled.

Throughout this manual the terms "area" or "neighborhood" are used interchangeably and refer to a readily identifiable portion of a community.

Whether this consists of so many blocks, an entire neighborhood, or a section thereof, it should be of such size as to permit the local code enforcement team to inspect and systematically effect minimum housing standards within a manageable time.

This means that area inspection programs involve systematic cellar-to-roof, house-to-house, block-to-block inspections of all properties within the specific area and include all the follow-up work required to bring the substandard housing up to code standards within a reasonable period. By putting major emphasis on this type of effort instead of on the complaint-oriented approach, blight is checked and an overall upgrading of residential sections is achieved in one portion of a community after another. Thus, systematic area inspection is both a longer lasting and a much more effective method of improving housing and stabilizing property values than the traditional complaint method.

Usually a municipality combines its area work with some complaint and referral inspections. This is not objectionable so long as major emphasis is given to the area programs, and the inspectors move through the various sections of town systematically. Only in this way can a community's housing inspection program contribute adequately to the municipal efforts to upgrade all substandard housing and stem the deterioration of individual homes and neighborhoods. A percentage of the inspection force should, however, be primarily assigned to complaint and referral work so that prompt action can be taken on all cases in which the problems are too severe to await action in connection with the area inspections.

While the area-wide or neighborhood inspections will correct violations of the housing code, this is all they will accomplish. Once these neighborhoods are brought up to standard, inspectors will move on to other neighborhoods but be forced to return at a later time and repeat the process.

If a neighborhood has declined to the extent that there is a large number of housing violations, then it is obvious that something or someone or both have caused the neighborhood to deteriorate. Any effort that does not also eliminate the cause for deterioration can only be a token effort and frequently a *wasted effort*. Unless a housing program evaluates the total neighborhood for both housing violations and for environmental stresses within the neighborhood that may have caused the deterioration of housing, then the inspectional effort has not been complete.

What then are these "environmental stresses"? Environmental stresses are the elements within a neighborhood that influence the physical, mental, and emotional well-being of the occupants. They include items such as noise, glare, excessive land covering, nonresidential land uses, and extensive traffic problems. If a housing program is to be complete, these stresses must be identified and assessed. Then efforts must be made in conjunction with other departments within the city to program capital improvement budgets to alleviate or minimize these stresses.

These two types of inspection are the field involvement of the housing inspector. He must inspect not only the houses for violations but also the neighborhoods for environmental stresses. This will provide him with knowledge of physical conditions within the neighborhood. As mentioned previously, however, this is not the whole problem in most neighborhoods. Generally, the very difficult problem of the human element is involved. Many buildings and neighborhoods deteriorate because of apathy on the part of the neighborhood inhabitants. Efforts must be made to motivate the slum dweller to work towards a better living environment. Experience by the Public Health Service (PHS) in motivational training has shown it to be very effective in raising the living standards of neighborhood populations.

In summary then, a housing inspection effort should be made up of three parts: First, a neighborhood or area-wide housing inspection procedure; second, a neighborhood analysis procedure to identify, assess, and eventually control environmental stresses; and third, a program of motivational training for slum dwellers to raise the living standards of the neighborhood.

III. Role of Health Agencies in Housing

Up until the end of World War II, most local housing hygiene programs were carried on by the health departments. After World War II, health agencies began to drift away from the field of housing hygiene. This gap was filled by a variety of other city agencies including building departments, police departments, fire departments, and more recently created departments of licenses and inspections. Regardless which department administers the housing code, the health department, if it is to live up to its responsibilities of protecting the public health, must have an involvement in housing. A general statement of PHS policy is that the basic responsibility of health agencies with regard to housing is to see to it that local and state governments take action to ensure that all occupied housing meets minimum public health standards. This basic responsibility falls upon federal, state, and local health agencies alike.

Several kinds of governmental action are required. These include: (1) adoption of minimum health standards in housing, (2) conduct of a program to achieve and maintain these standards, (3) periodic evaluation of the standards to ensure their current adequacy, and (4) monitoring of the standards enforcement effort to guarantee that public health values are provided. Health agencies, in order to meet their responsibilities, must accept the role of either stimulating or carrying out these four required kinds of governmental action.

In communities that have neither standards nor program, the health agency has the responsibility of initiating both by stimulating the required governmental action. Stimulation may be direct, through elected or appointed officials, or indirect, by generating public support that will trigger official action.

IV. Summary

Several basic thoughts are contained in this chapter.

1. Housing is an old, well-established but often overlooked topic within this country. Indications are, however, that the broad field of housing will receive much more attention from the policymakers throughout the country within the coming years.

2. No single agency can eliminate urban blight. A concentrated effort of all city departments, private concerns, and political bodies must be focused on small sections (neighborhoods) to minimize or control urban blight and its associated human sufferings.

3. A housing effort cannot be successful if it is merely an inspection of houses for code compliance. There must also be a united effort to eliminate environmental stresses within the neighborhood and instill motivation in slum dwellers to desire and work towards improving their environment.

GLOSSARY OF REAL ESTATE TERMS

TABLE OF CONTENTS

	Page
Abstract of Title ... Alienation	1
Amortization ... Avulsion	2
Beneficiary ... Cease and Desist Order	3
Cease and Desist Petition ... Conversion	4
Conveyance ... Depreciation	5
Descent ... Equity	6
Equity of Redemption ... Exclusive Right to Sell	7
Executor ... Gross Lease	8
Ground Rent ... Jeopardy	9
Joint Tenancy ... Mandatory	10
Market Value ... Multiple Listing	11
Net Listing ... Personal Property	12
Plat Book ... Recording	13
Redemption ... Set Back	14
Severalty ... Tenancy at Will	15
Tenant ... Voidable	16
Waiver ... Zoning Ordinance	17

GLOSSARY OF REAL ESTATE TERMS

A

Abstract of Title - A summary of all of the recorded instruments and proceedings which affect the title to property, arranged in chronological order.

Accretion - The addition to land through processes of nature, as by streams or wind.

Accrued Interest - Accrue: to grow; to be added to. Accrued interest is interest that has been earned but not due and payable.

Acknowledgment - A formal declaration before a duly authorized officer by a person who has executed an instrument that such execution is the person's act and deed.

Acquisition- An act or process by which a person procures property.

Acre - A measure of land equaling 160 square rods or 4,840 square yards or 43,560 feet.

Adjacent - Lying near to but not necessarily in actual contact with.

Adjoining - Contiguous; attaching, in actual contact with.

Administrator - A person appointed by court to administer the estate of a deceased person who left no will; i.e., who died intestate.

Ad Valorem - According to valuation.

Adverse Possession - A means of acquiring title where an occupant has been in actual, open, notorious, exclusive, and continuous occupancy of property under a claim of right for the required statutory period.

Affidavit - A statement or declaration reduced to writing, and sworn to or affirmed before some officer who is authorized to administer an oath or affirmation.

Affirm - To confirm, to ratify, to verify.

Agency - That relationship between principal and agent which arises out of a contract either expressed or implied, written or oral, wherein an agent is employed by a person to do certain acts on the person's behalf in dealing with a third party.

Agent - One who undertakes to transact some business or to manage some affair for another by authority of the latter.

Agreement of Sale - A written agreement between seller and purchaser in which the purchaser agrees to buy certain real estate and the seller agrees to sell upon terms and conditions set forth therein.

Alienation - A transferring of property to another; the transfer of property and possession of lands, or other things, from one person to another.

Amortization - A gradual paying off of a debt by periodical installments.

Apportionments - Adjustment of the income, expenses or carrying charges of real estate usually computed to the date of closing of title so that the seller pays all expenses to that date. The buyer assumes all expenses commencing the date the deed is conveyed to the buyer.

Appraisal - An estimate of a property's valuation by an appraiser who is usually presumed to be expert in this work.

Appraisal by Capitalization - An estimate of value by capitalization of productivity and income.

Appraisal by Comparison - Comparability with the sale prices of other similar properties.

Appraisal by Summation - Adding together all parts of a property separately appraised to form a whole: e.g., value of the land considered as vacant added to the cost of reproduction of the building, less depreciation.

Appurtenance - Something which is outside the property itself but belongs to the land and adds to its greater enjoyment such as a right of way or a barn or a dwelling.

Assessed Valuation - A valuation placed upon property by a public officer or a board, as a basis for taxation.

Assessment - A charge against real estate made by a unit of government to cover a proportionate cost of an improvement such as a street or sewer.

Assessor - An official who has the responsibility of determining assessed values.

Assignee - The person to whom an agreement or contract is assigned.

Assignment - The method or manner by which a right, a specialty, or contract is transferred from one person to another.

Assignor - A party who assigns or transfers an agreement or contract to another.

Assumption of Mortgage - The taking of title to property by a grantee, wherein the grantee assumes liability for payment of an existing note or bond secured by a mortgage against a property and becomes personally liable for the payment of such mortgage debt.

Attest - To witness to; to witness by observation and signature.

Avulsion - The removal of land from one owner to another, when a stream suddenly changes its channel.

B

Beneficiary - The person who receives or is to receive the benefits resulting from certain acts.

Bequeath - To give or hand down by will; to leave by will.

Bequest - That which is given by the terms of a will.

Bill of Sale - A written instrument given to pass title of personal property from vendor to vendee.

Binder - An agreement to cover the down payment for the purchase of real estate as evidence of good faith on the part of the purchaser.

Blanket Mortgage - A single mortgage which covers more than one piece of real estate.

Bona Fide - In good faith, without fraud.

Bond - The evidence of a personal debt which is secured by a mortgage or other lien on real estate.

Building Codes - Regulations established by local governments stating fully the structural requirements for building.

Building Line - A line fixed at a certain distance from the front and/or sides of a lot, beyond which no building can project.

Building Loan Agreement - An agreement whereby the lender advances money to an owner with provisional payments at certain stages of construction.

C

Cancellation Clause - A provision in a lease which confers upon One or more or all of the parties to the lease the right to terminate the party's or parties' obligations thereunder upon the occurrence of the condition or contingency set forth in the said clause.

Caveat Emptor - Let the buyer beware. The buyer must examine the goods or property and buy at the buyer's own risk.

Cease and Desist Order - An order executed by the Secretary of State directing broker recipients to cease and desist from all solicitation of homeowners whose names and addresses appear on the list(s) forwarded with such order.
The order acknowledges petition filings by homeowners listed evidencing their premises are not for sale, thereby revoking the implied invitation to solicit.
The issuance of a Cease and Desist Order does not prevent an owner from selling or listing his premises for sale. It prohibits soliciting by licensees served with such order and subjects violators to penalties of suspension or revocation of their licenses as provided in section 441-c of the Real Property Law.

Cease and Desist Petition - A statement filed by a homeowner showing address of premises owned which notifies the Department of State that such premises are not for sale and does not wish to be solicited. In so doing, petitioner revokes the implied invitation to be solicited, by any means with respect thereto, by licensed real estate brokers and salespersons.

Certiorari - A proceeding to review in a competent court the action of an inferior tribunal board or officer exercising judicial functions.

Chain of Title - A history of conveyances and encumbrances affecting a title from the time the original patent was granted, or as far back as records are available.

Chattel - Personal property, such as household goods or fixtures.

Chattel Mortgage - A mortgage on personal property.

Client - The one by whom a broker is employed and by whom the broker will be compensated on completion of the purpose of the agency.

Closing Date - The date upon which the buyer takes over the property; usually between 30 and 60 days after the signing of the contract.

Cloud on the Title - An outstanding claim or encumbrance which, if valid, would affect or impair the owner's title.

Collateral - Additional security pledged for the payment of an obligation.

Color of Title - That which appears to be good title, but which is not title in fact.

Commission - A sum due a real estate broker for services in that capacity.

Commitment - A pledge or a promise or affirmation agreement.

Condemnation - Taking private property for public use, with fair compensation to the owner; exercising the right of eminent domain.

Conditional Sales Contract - A contract for the sale of property stating that delivery is to be made to the buyer, title to remain vested in the seller until the conditions of the contract have been fulfilled.

Consideration - Anything of value given to induce entering into a contract; it may be money, personal services, or even love and affection.

Constructive Notice - Information or knowledge of a fact imputed by law to a person because the person could have discovered the fact by proper diligence and inquiry; (public records).

Contract - An agreement between competent parties to do or not to do certain things for a legal consideration, whereby each party acquires a right to what the other possesses.

Conversion - Change from one character or use to another.

Conveyance - The transfer of the title of land from one to another. The means or medium by which title of real estate is transferred.

County Clerk's Certificate - When an acknowledgment is taken by an officer not authorized in the state or county where the document is to be recorded, the instrument which must be attached to the acknowledgment is called a county clerk's certificate. It is given by the clerk of the county where the officer obtained his/her authority and certifies to the officer's signature and powers.

Covenants - Agreements written into deeds and other instruments promising performance or nonperformance of certain acts, or stipulating certain uses or nonuses of the property.

D

Damages - The indemnity recoverable by a person who has sustained an injury, either to his/her person, property or relative rights, through the art or default of another.

Decedent - One who is dead.

Decree - Order issued by one in authority; an edirt or law; a judicial decision.

Dedication - A grant and appropriation of land by its owner for some public use, accepted for such use, by an authorized public official on behalf of the public.

Deed - An instrument in writing duly executed and delivered, that conveys title to real property.

Deed Restriction - An imposed restriction in a deed for the purpose of limiting the use of the land such as:
1. A restriction against the sale of liquor thereon.
2. A restriction as to the size, type, value or placement of improvements that may be erected thereon.

Default - Failure to fulfill a duty or promise, or to discharge an obligation; omission or failure to perform any acts.

Defendant - The party sued or called to answer in any suit, civil or criminal, at law or in equity.

Deficiency Judgment - A judgment given when the security for a loan does not entirely satisfy the debt upon its default.

Delivery - The transfer of the possession of a thing from one person to another.

Demising Clause - A clause found in a lease whereby the landlord (lessor) leases and the tenant (lessee) takes the property.

Depreciation - Loss of value in real property brought about by age, physical deterioration, or functional or economic obsolescence.

Descent - When an owner of real estate dies intestate, the owner's property descends, by operation of law, to the owner's distributees.

Devise - A gift of real estate by will or last testament.

Devisee - One who receives a bequest of real estate made by will.

Devisor - One who bequeaths real estate by will.

Directional Growth - The location or direction toward which the residential sections of a city are destined or determined to grow.

Dispossess Proceedings - Summary process by a landlord to oust a tenant and regain possession of the premises for nonpayment of rent or other breach of conditions of the lease or occupancy.

Distributee - Person receiving or entitled to receive land as representative of the former owner.

Documentary Evidence - Evidence in the form of written or printed papers.

Duress - Unlawful constraint exercised upon a person whereby the person is forced to do some act against his will.

E

Earnest Money - Down payment made by a purchaser of real estate as evidence of good faith.

Easement - A right that may be exercised by the public or individuals on, over or through the lands of others.

Ejectment - A form of action to regain possession of real property, with damages for the unlawful retention; used when there is no relationship of landlord and tenant.

Eminent Domain - A right of the government to acquire property for necessary public use by condemnation; the owner must be fairly compensated.

Encroachment - A building, part of a building, or obstruction which intrudes upon or invades a highway or sidewalk or trespasses upon the property of another.

Encumbrance - Any right to or interest in land that diminishes its value. *(Also Incumbrance)*

Endorsement - An act of signing one's name on the back of a check or note, with or without further qualifications.

Equity - The interest or value which the owner has in real estate over and above the liens against it.

Equity of Redemption - A right of the owner to reclaim property before it is sold through foreclosure proceedings, by the payment of the debt, interest and costs.

Erosion - The wearing away of land through processes of nature, as by streams and winds.

Escheat - The reversion to the state of property in event the owner thereof dies, without leaving a will and has no distributees to whom the property may pass by lawful descent.

Escrow - A written agreement between two or more parties providing that certain instruments or property be placed with a third party to be delivered to a designated person upon the fulfillment or performance of some act or condition.

Estate - The degree, quantity, nature and extent of interest which a person has in real property.

Estate for Life - An estate or interest held during the terms of some certain person's life.

Estate in Reversion - The residue of an estate left for the grantor, to commence in possession after the termination of some particular estate granted by the grantor.

Estate at Will - The occupation of lands and tenements by a tenant for an indefinite period, terminable by one or both parties at will.

Estoppel Certificate - An instrument executed by the mortgagor setting forth the present status and the balance due on the mortgage as of the date of the execution of the certificate.

Eviction - A legal proceeding by a lessor landlord to recover possession of real property.

Eviction, Actual - Where one is, either by force or by process of law, actually put out of possession.

Eviction, Constructive - Any disturbance of the tenant's possessions by the landlord whereby the premises are rendered unfit or unsuitable for the purpose for which they were leased.

Eviction, Partial - Where the possessor of the premises is deprived of a portion thereof.

Exclusive Agency - An agreement of employment of a broker to the exclusion of all other brokers; if sale is made by any other broker during term of employment, broker holding exclusive agency is entitled to commissions in addition to the commissions payable to the broker who effected the transaction.

Exclusive Right to Sell - An agreement of employment by a broker under which the exclusive right to sell for a specified period is granted to the broker; if a sale during the term of the agreement is made by the owner or by any other broker, the broker holding such exclusive right to sell is nevertheless entitled to compensation.

Executor - A male person or a corporate entity or any other type of organization named or designated in a will to carry out its provisions as to the disposition of the estate of a deceased person.

Executrix - A woman appointed to perform the duties similar to those of an executor.

Extension Agreement - An agreement which extends the life of a mortgage to a later date.

F

Fee; Fee Simple; Fee Absolute - Absolute ownership of real property; a person has this type of estate where the person is entitled to the entire property with unconditional power of disposition during the person's life and descending to the person's distributees and legal representatives upon the person's death intestate.

Fiduciary - A person who on behalf of or for the benefit of another transacts business or handles money on property not the person's own; such relationship implies great confidence and trust.

Fixtures - Personal property so attached to the land or improvements as to become part of the real property.

Foreclosure - A procedure whereby property pledged as security for a debt is sold to pay the debt in the event of default in payments or terms.

Forfeiture - Loss of money or anything of value, by way of penalty due to failure to perform.

Freehold - An interest in real estate, not less than an estate for life. (Use of this term discontinued Sept. 1, 1967.)

Front Foot - A standard measurement, one foot wide, of the width of land, applied at the frontage on its street line. Each front foot extends the depth of the lot.

G

Grace Period - Additional time allowed to perform an act or make a payment before a default occurs.

Graduated Leases - A lease which provides for a graduated change at stated intervals in the amount of the rent to be paid; used largely in long term leases.

Grant - A technical term used in deeds of conveyance of lands to indicate a transfer.

Grantee - The party to whom the title to real property is conveyed.

Grantor - The person who conveys real estate by deed; the seller.

Gross Income - Total income from property before any expenses are deducted.

Gross Lease - A lease of property whereby the lessor is to meet all property charges regularly incurred through ownership.

Ground Rent - Earnings of improved property credited to earning of the ground itself after allowance made for earnings of improvements.

H

Habendum Clause - The "To Have and To Hold" clause which defines or limits the quantity of the estate granted in the premises of the deed.

Hereditaments - The largest classification of property; including lands, tenements and incorporeal property, such as rights of way.

Holdover Tenant - A tenant who remains in possession of leased property after the expiration of the lease term.

Hypothecate - To give a thing as security without the necessity of giving up possession of it.

I

In Rem - A proceeding against the realty directly; as distinguished from a proceeding against a person. (Used in taking land for nonpayment of taxes, etc.)

Incompetent - A person who is unable to manage his/her own affairs by reason of insanity, inbecility or feeble-mindedness.

Incumbrance - Any right to or interest in land that diminishes its value. *(Also Encumbrance)*

Injunction - A writ or order issued under the seal of a court to restrain one or more parties to a suit or proceeding from doing an act which is deemed to be inequitable or unjust in regard to the rights of some other party or parties in the suit or proceeding.

Installments - Parts of the same debt, payable at successive periods as agreed; payments made to reduce a mortgage.

Instrument - A written legal document; created to effect the rights of the parties.

Interest Rate - The percentage of a sum of money charged for its use.

Intestate - A person who dies having made no will, or leaves one which is defective in form, in which case the person's estate descends to the person's distributees.

Involuntary Lien - A lien imposed against property without consent of the owner, i.e., taxes, special assessments.

Irrevocable - Incapable of being recalled or revoked; unchangeable; unalterable.

J

Jeopardy - Peril, danger.

Joint Tenancy - Ownership of realty by two or more persons, each of whom has an undivided interest with the "right of survivorship."

Judgment - Decree of a court declaring that one individual is indebted to another, and fixing the amount of such indebtedness.

Junior Mortgage - A mortgage second in lien to a previous mortgage.

L

Laches - Delay or negligence in asserting one's legal rights.

Land, Tenements and Hereditaments - A phrase used in the early English Law, to express all sorts of property of the immovable class.

Landlord - One who rents property to another.

Lease - A contract whereby, for a consideration, usually termed rent, one who is entitled to the possession of real property transfers such rights to another for life, for a term of years, or at will.

Leasehold - The interest or estate which a lessee of real estate has therein by virtue of the lessee's lease.

Lessee - A person to whom property is rented under a lease.

Lessor - One who rents property to another under a lease.

Lien - A legal right or claim upon a specific property which attaches to the property until a debt is satisfied.

Lien (Mechanic's) - A notice filed with the County Clerk stating that payment has not been made for an improvement to real property.

Life Estate - The conveyance of title to property for the duration of the life of the grantee.

Life Tenant - The holder of a life estate.

Lis Pendens - A legal document, filed in the office of the county clerk giving notice that an action or proceeding is pending in the courts affecting the title to the property.

Listing - An employment contract between principal and agent, authorizing the agent to perform services for the principal involving the latter's property.

Litigation - The act of carrying on a lawsuit.

M

Mandatory - Requiring strict conformity or obedience.

Market Value - The highest price which a buyer, willing but not compelled to buy, would pay, and the lowest a seller, willing but not compelled to sell, would accept.

Marketable Title - A title which a court of equity considers to be so free from defect that it will enforce its acceptance by a purchaser.

Mechanic's Lien - A lien given by law upon a building or other improvement upon land, and upon the land itself, to secure the price of labor done upon, and materials furnished for. the improvement.

Meeting of the Minds - Whenever all parties to a contract agree to the exact terms thereof.

Metes and Bounds - A term used in describing the boundary lines of land, setting forth all the boundary lines together with their terminal points and angles.

Minor - A person under an age specified by law; under 18 years of age.

Monument - A fixed object and point established by surveyors to establish land locations.

Moratorium - An emergency act by a legislative body to suspend the legal enforcement of contractual obligations.

Mortgage - An instrument in writing, duly executed and delivered, that creates a lien upon real estate as security for the payment of a specified debt, which is usually in the form of a bond.

Mortgage Commitment - A formal indication, by a lending institution that it will grant a mortgage loan on property, in a certain specified amount and on certain specified terms.

Mortgage Reduction Certificate - An instrument executed by the mortgagee, setting forth the present status and the balance due on the mortgage as of the date of the execution of the instrument.

Mortgagee - The party who lends money and takes a mortgage to secure the payment thereof.

Mortgagor - A person who borrows money and gives a mortgage on the person's property as security for the payment of the debt.

Multiple Listing - An arrangement among Real Estate Board of Exchange Members, whereby each broker presents the broker's listings to the attention of the other members so that if a sale results, the commission is divided between the broker bringing the listing and the broker making the sale.

N

Net Listing - A price below which an owner will not sell the property, and at which price a broker will not receive a commission; the broker receives the excess over and above the net listing as the broker's commission.

Notary Public - A public officer who is authorized to take acknowledgments to certain classes of documents, such as deeds, contracts, mortgages, and before whom affidavits may be sworn.

O

Obligee - The person in whose favor an obligation is entered into.

Obligor - The person who binds himself/herself to another; one who has engaged to perform some obligation; one who makes a bond.

Obsolescence - Loss in value due to reduced desirability and usefulness of a structure because its design and construction become obsolete; loss because of becoming old-fashioned, and not in keeping with modern means, with consequent loss of income.

Open End Mortgage - A mortgage under which the mortgagor may secure additional funds from the mortgagee, usually up to but not exceeding the original amount of the existing amortizing mortgage.

Open Listing - A listing given to any number of brokers without liability to compensate any except the one who first secures a buyer ready, willing and able to meet the terms of the listing, or secures the acceptance by the seller of a satisfactory offer; the sale of the property automatically terminates the listing.

Open Mortgage - A mortgage that has matured or is overdue and, therefore, is "open" to foreclosure at any time.

Option - A right given for a consideration to purchase or lease a property upon specified terms within a specified time; if the right is not exercised the option holder is not subject to liability for damages; if exercised, the grantor of option must perform.

P

Partition - The division which is made of real property between those who own it in undivided shares.

Party Wall - A party wall is a wall built along the line separating two properties, partly on each, which wall either owner, the owner's heirs and assigns has the right to use; such right constituting an easement over so much of the adjoining owner's land as is covered by the wall.

Percentage Lease - A lease of property in which the rental is based upon the percentage of the volume of sales made upon the leased premises, usually provides for minimum rental.

Personal Property - Any property which is not real property.

Plat Book - A public record containing maps of land showing the division of such land into streets, blocks and lots and indicating the measurements of the individual parcels.

Plottage - Increment in unity value of a plot of land created by assembling smaller ownerships into one ownership.

Police Power - The right of any political body to enact laws and enforce them, for the order, safety, health, morals and general welfare of the public.

Power of Attorney - A written instrument duly signed and executed by an owner of property, which authorizes an agent to act on behalf of the owner to the extent indicated in the instrument.

Premises - Lands and tenements; an estate; the subject matter of a conveyance.

Prepayment Clause - A clause in a mortgage which gives a mortgagor the privilege of paying the mortgage indebtedness before it becomes due.

Principal - The employer of an agent or broker; the broker's or agent's client.

Probate - To establish the will of a deceased person.

Purchase Money Mortgage - A mortgage given by a grantee in part payment of the purchase price of real estate.

Q

Quiet Enjoyment - The right of an owner or a person legally in possession to the use of property without interference of possession.

Quiet Title Suit - A suit in court to remove a defect, cloud or suspicion regarding legal rights of an owner to a certain parcel of real property.

Quitclaim Deed - A deed which conveys simply the grantor's rights or interest in real estate, without any agreement or covenant as to the nature or extent of that interest, or any other covenants; usually used to remove a cloud from the title.

R

Real Estate Board - An organization whose members consist primarily of real estate brokers and salespersons.

Real Property - Land, and generally whatever is erected upon or affixed thereto.

Realtor - A coined word which may only be used by an active member of a local real estate board, affiliated with the National Association of Real Estate Boards.

Recording - The act of writing or entering in a book of public record instruments affecting the title to real property.

Redemption - The right of a mortgagor to redeem the property by paying a debt after the expiration date and before sale at foreclosure; the right of an owner to reclaim the owner's property after the sale for taxes.

Release - The act or writing by which some claim or interest is surrendered to another.

Release Clause - A clause found in a blanket mortgage which gives the owner of the property the privilege of paying off a portion of the mortgage indebtedness, and thus freeing a portion of the property from the mortgage.

Rem - *(See In Rem)*

Remainder - An estate which takes effect after the termination of a prior estate such as a life estate.

Remainderman - The person who is to receive the property after the death of a life tenant.

Rent - The compensation paid for the use of real estate.

Reproduction Cost - Normal cost of exact duplication of a property as of a certain date.

Restriction - A limitation placed upon the use of property contained in the deed or other written instrument in the chain of title.

Reversionary Interest - The interest which a person has in lands or other property upon the termination of the preceding estate.

Revocation - An act of recalling a power of authority conferred, as the revocation of a power of attorney, a license, an agency, etc.

Right of Survivorship - Right of the surviving joint owner to succeed to the interests of the deceased joint owner, distinguishing feature of a joint tenancy or tenancy by the entirety.

Right of Way - The right to pass over another's land more or less frequently according to the nature of the easement.

Riparian Owner - One who owns land bounding upon a river or watercourse.

Riparian Rights - The right of a landowner to water on, under or adjacent to his land.

S

Sales Contract - A contract by which the buyer and seller agree to terms of sale.

Satisfaction Piece - An instrument for recording and acknowledging payment of an indebtedness secured by a mortgage.

Seizin - The possession of land by one who claims to own at least an estate for life therein.

Set Back - The distance from the curb or other established line, within which no buildings may be erected.

Severalty - The ownership of real property by an individual, as an individual.

Special Assessment - An assessment made against a property to pay for a public improvement by which the assessed property is supposed to be especially benefited.

Specific Performance - A remedy in a court of equity compelling a defendant to carry out the terms of an agreement or contract.

Statute - A law established by an act of the Legislature.

Statute of Frauds - State law which provides that certain contracts must be in writing in order to be enforceable at law.

Stipulations - The terms within a written contract.

Straight Line Depreciation - A definite sum set aside annually from income to pay costs of replacing improvements, without reference to the interest it earns.

Subdivision - A tract of land divided into lots or plots suitable for home building purposes.

Subletting - A leasing by a tenant to another, who holds under the tenant.

Subordination Clause - A clause which permits the placing of a mortgage at a later date which takes priority over an existing mortgage.

Subscribing Witness - One who writes his/her name as witness to the execution of an instrument.

Surety - One who guarantees the performance of another; guarantor.

Surrender - The cancellation of a lease by mutual consent of the lessor and the lessee.

Surrogate's Court (Probate Court) - A court having jurisdiction over the proof of wills, the settling of estates and of citations.

Survey - The process by which a parcel of land is measured and its area ascertained; also the blueprint showing the measurements, boundaries and area.

T

Tax Sale - Sale of property after a period of nonpayment of taxes.

Tenancy in Common - An ownership of realty by two or more persons, each of whom has an undivided interest, without the "right of survivorship."

Tenancy by the Entirety - An estate which exists only between husband and wife with equal right of possession and enjoyment during their joint lives and with the "right of survivorship."

Tenancy at Will - A license to use or occupy lands and tenements at the will of the owner.

Tenant - One who is given possession of real estate for a fixed period or at will.

Tenant at Sufferance - One who comes into possession of lands by lawful title and keeps it afterwards without any title at all.

Testate - Where a person dies leaving a valid will.

Title - Evidence that owner of land is in lawful possession thereof; evidence of ownership.

Title Insurance - A policy of insurance which indemnifies the holder for any loss sustained by reason of defects in the title.

Title Search - An examination of the public records to determine the ownership and encumbrances affecting real property.

Torrens Title - System of title records provided by state law; it is a system for the registration of land titles whereby the state of the title, showing ownership and encumbrances, can be readily ascertained from an inspection of the "register of titles" without the necessity of a search of the public records.

Tort - A wrongful act, wrong, injury; violation of a legal right.

Transfer Tax - A tax charged under certain conditions on the property belonging to an estate.

U

Unearned Increment - An increase in value of real estate due to no effort on the part of the owner: often due to increase in population.

Urban Property - City property; closely settled property.

Usury - On a loan, claiming a rate of interest greater than that permitted by law.

V

Valid - Having force, or binding force; legally sufficient and authorized by law.

Valuation - Estimated worth or price. The art of valuing by appraisal.

Vendee's Lien - A lien against property under contract of sale to secure deposit paid by a purchaser.

Verification - Sworn statements before a duly qualified officer to the correctness of the contents of an instrument.

Violations - Act, deed or conditions contrary to law or permissible use of real property.

Void - To have no force or effect; that which is unenforceable.

Voidable - That which is capable of being adjudged void, but is not void unless action is taken to make it so.

W

Waiver - The renunciation, abandonment or surrender of some claim, right or privilege.

Warranty Deed - A conveyance of land in which the grantor warrants the title to the grantee.

Will - The disposition of one's property to take effect after death.

Without - RecourseWords used in endorsing a note or bill to denote that the future holder is not co look to the endorser in case of nonpayment.

Z

Zone - An area set off by the proper authorities for specific use; subject to certain restrictions or restraints.

Zoning Ordinance - Act of city or county or other authorities specifying type and use to which property may be put in specific areas.